An end to factory schools

An education manifesto 2010-2020

ANTHONY SELDON

THE AUTHOR

Anthony Seldon is the Master at Wellington College and, before that, was headmaster of Brighton College. He is author or editor of 25 books and is the biographer of John Major and Tony Blair and, next, Gordon Brown. His most recent book was *Trust* (Biteback, 2009).

Support towards research for this Study was given by the Institute for Policy Research.

ISBN No. 978-1-906996-19-2

Printed by 4 Print, 138 Molesey Avenue, Surrey

CONTENTS

DEDICATION

To my courageous mother, Marjorie Seldon, an early and eloquent champion of education vouchers and parental choice.

PREFACE

Schools should be places of engagement and delight. Instead, students often resent and insufficiently value them. Parents should be actively engaged in and full of gratitude for the schools that their children attend. Instead, they are often indifferent and even unco-operative. Teaching should be a profession which the brightest and most energetic should aspire to and fight to join. Instead, it is hard to get top graduates to apply. And when they do, it is hard to keep them in the profession (which is a profession in name alone). To be a head should be the apex of every teacher's dream. Instead, such is the encumbered nature of the job, many heads' posts remain unfilled.

Too many state schools in Britain in 2010 have become factories. Results (at least on paper) have improved. But at what cost? Reluctant students are processed through a system which is closely controlled and monitored by the state. No area of public life is more important than education to prepare people to live meaningful, productive and valuable lives. Yet our schools turn out young people who are often incapable of living full and autonomous lives. At the same time, employers condemn students' lack of academic and personal skills while universities find that the end products of schools can be little more than well-drilled automatons who do not know how to think independently about their academic subjects.

Five reasons why education needs to change

The traditional model for education is no longer working.

1. **Finance.** The unprecedented increase in spending under Labour on schools of £30 billion a year, at an annual average rate of increase of 6.8%, has failed to improve standards commensurately (measured by exam results and attendance rates), according to the Office of National Statistics.[1] Conventional funding streams from government will come under great pressure in the immediate future. But money is not of itself the solution to the problems facing our schools: many of the proposals made here do not require extra funds.

2. **Holistic development.** Schools have major responsibilities for developing the whole person, not just their intellect. The traditional model of large, de-personalised and exam-focused schools is appropriate neither for the academic, cultural, moral, spiritual, physical and emotional development of young people, nor for preparing them for a fruitful life.

3. **The demands of tomorrow.** The new world does not need container loads of young men and women whose knowledge is narrowly academic and subject-specific which they can regurgitate in splendid isolation in exams. It needs people who have genuine understanding not just in one but in several academic domains, and who comprehend how these different

---

[1] ONS, *Education and Training Statistics for the United Kingdom: 2009*, 2009.

fields relate to each other. It needs people who can work collaboratively, with advanced interpersonal skills, as opposed to those who have been tested merely on their ability to write exam answers on their own. It needs problem solvers rather than those who just hold a large body of data in their memories. It needs employees who will have mature thinking skills, able to understand the complexity and the interaction of intricate systems, people who are able to think way beyond standard and formulaic patterns. It is no longer good enough to continue to argue that 'the twenty first century, with its accelerating pace of change, will be unknowable'. We have already seen enough of it to be able to know that we need dramatically to adapt our schools.[2]

4. **Information and communication technology.** ICT is revolutionising the classroom and learning more than any other development in the last 200 years. It has already had a profound effect on administration within schools, but has barely touched teaching and learning. Today, many teachers are still using it merely as a more sophisticated version of chalk and blackboard. In the new era, teachers will no longer be the fonts and dispensers of all knowledge, but rather expert collaborators assisting and guiding the young in their own research and academic development. Learning will become much more centred on problem-solving, collaborative activities, the mixing of ages and advancing at a pace suitable for each child. This quantum shift will be profoundly liberating and enriching, but has yet to be made in most schools. We have yet to get fully to grip too, with young people's intimacy with digital technologies, and the influences it has on their

---

[2]   See Damian Allen, *Evidence to the PCSE great schools enquiry*, 7 July 2009.

intellectual development and cognitive skills. Bringing the curriculum and exams in line with where students currently are with digital technology, let alone where they will be in ten years, is a major challenge. All that said, some of the best teaching and learning will remain utterly divorced from anything digital.

5. **Research on the brain**. Although still in its infancy, research is already reaching some important conclusions about learning. These are discussed throughout the booklet, but a sample of the points made are as follows. Emotional receptivity, humour and human warmth are powerful facilitators to learning. Arid teaching and lecturing from the front of the classroom is not optimal (and further suggests the computer will never take replace the teacher). Physiological cycles and environmental factors on the brain affect learning and how the mind takes in and stores information. Active and practical learning, research shows, is more effective than passive, because the brain is more stimulated. Pupils can often learn more from teaching each other than from teachers. The young can be taught at school about resilience and self-discipline,[3] which is a powerful shaper of the effectiveness of that person when they become an adult. The research shows us that 'IQ' is not fixed, and that children hitherto dismissed as 'low ability' can learn and improve: this finding about 'neuro-plasticity' has profound implications for schools. The more that educators can learn how the brain functions, the better they will be able to cater for and stimulate students.

---

[3] See Angela Duckworth and Martin Seligman, 'Self-discipline gives girls the edge', *Journal of educational psychology*, 2006, volume 98, no. 1, pp 198-208. See also Paul Tough, 'Can the right kinds of play teach self control?', *New York Times Magazine*, 25 September 2009.

Schools in 2010 are full of remarkable teachers, and hard working students who, sometimes, achieve extraordinary results on slender resources. But the present reality falls far short of what schools could and should be.

If one unifying idea draws together the ensuing chapters, it is the need for more *trust* throughout education.[4] Government needs to trust schools, heads and teachers more. Parents need to be trusted more to choose the school for their children and to be far more actively involved in their children's schools. Governors need to trust heads more. Heads need to trust teachers more. Teachers need to trust students more. Parents need to trust their children more. Students need to trust adults more. Mistakes will be made, but that in a free society is how learning occurs, how progress is made.

Many of the same phenomena addressed here apply to universities as much as they do to schools. There, too, individual students are obliged to meet the requirements of a pedestrian exam monolith, creative teaching is sacrificed to instruction and transmitting the right or approved answers and students have an increasingly narrow quality of all-round education as higher education increasingly loses sight of its mission to educate the whole student.

Delight, gratitide and stiumulus can readily be recaptured throughout education if the prescriptions made here are followed. To educate the young to lead a full and whole life should be the sovereign duty of every school. It is one which should no longer be ducked.

---

[4]   Antony Seldon, *Trust: How we lost it, and how to get it back,* Biteback, 2009.

1. TWENTY RECOMMENDATIONS

1. **Genuinely independent state schools**. All schools should become legally autonomous within five years if they show themselves to be worthy of handling independence. The vast majority will be able to do this. They would still be subject to the principle of 'accountable autonomy' but independence should only be denied or reclaimed from those schools which are conspicuously failing their pupils. Heads would be able to decide matters such as the curriculum, school size, admissions procedures, discipline policies, the hours staff should work and whether their schools should be co-educational.

2. **Curriculum autonomy.** Schools should be free to decide their own curriculum, and the way that it is taught. The role of government should be limited to ensuring that minimum levels of attainment are reached at the end of each key stage and that all children are taught mainstream academic subjects until the age of 14.

3. **Intellectual rigour.** At present, intellectual depth is lacking in too many schools. Those schools which wish to have freedom over their curriculum will need to show that they

give serious weight to the development of each child's intellectual needs.

4. **Active learning not rote learning.** In too many schools there are insufficient opportunities for students to think and learn independently. Allowing students to explore solutions themselves before being told the answer by the teacher helps them to become active learners. Experiments by students in science could be far more widespread.

5. **Holistic development.** Few state schools offer the same opportunities for holistic education as independent schools. They should be encouraged to provide opportunities for all children to develop all 'eight aptitudes'. A good curriculum should also develop each child's personal qualities, as does the International Baccalaureate's (IB) 'learner profile' and in the IB's 'areas of interaction'. The school day could be lengthened to allow more time for such enrichment.

6. **Behaviour and wellbeing.** Schools should have high expectations of all children. Schools should be free to adopt their own behaviour regime, where good behaviour, and zero tolerance of poor behaviour should be constantly reinforced. Promoting 'well-being' does not require special lessons, but could be emphasised in all aspects of a school's activities, including politeness and good manners, and a smart and distinct school uniform.

7. **Service.** Schools can provide the opportunity for children to be active in volunteering and serving others within the community. Students, schools and the wider society would all benefit from schools offering 'combined cadet forces' to students aged between 14 and 16, and from providing opportunities for outdoor adventure, expeditions and challenge.

8. **Pupil responsibility.** Students can be trusted far more. Every student would gain from being given positions of responsibility before they leave school. Schools could be much more imaginative and courageous in realising that students are capable of far more responsibility and leadership than they are currently given.

9. **Diversify public examinations.** The current exam regime should be restructured, and the stranglehold of A-Levels and GCSEs in England and Wales should be ended. Government should welcome alternative exam systems, including the IB at diploma, middle years and primary years level. Within schools, the focus should shift away from assessment and teaching-to-the test, towards genuine learning and understanding. The influence of QCDA and Ofqual should be greatly reduced. Universities should be more involved in the development of examinations of all kinds, above all in the sixth form.

10. **League Tables.** Simplistic league tables which take no account of the quality of the intake of the school should be sidelined in favour of genuine value-added league tables. They should be designed to reveal information which is genuinely useful for parents and others to make discriminating judgements.

11. **Inspection.** The current inspection regime should be replaced. Schools which are performing poorly should be inspected regularly, while those performing at high levels should not be inspected at all. Ofsted should be cut considerably and be focused on teaching and learning, not on children's services. Serving teachers should be used in inspection teams with up to half of them composed of teachers on secondment annually for the week of the

inspection. Teachers considered to be 'very good' or 'excellent' should be encouraged to take part in one school inspection a year.

12. **Facilitating teacher recruitment.** Pathways into teaching must be made easier for able and highly committed graduates. There should be less emphasis on theory for postgraduates, and easier entry into teaching for those who have already built careers outside the profession. 'Teach First' has helped make the profession more attractive, and needs to become 'Teach Second' and 'Teach Third'.

13. **Make schools more congenial for teachers.** Teachers will never receive high salaries compared to many other professions. But a congenial environment can compensate. Teachers need to spend less time on bureaucracy (reducing government interference will slash bureaucracy dramatically) so they can concentrate on what they do best, which is to teach and develop young people inside and outside the classroom.

14. **Discipline.** Successful schools have tight discipline. Classrooms, corridors and public spaces in schools should be places of order where no teacher or child feels fearful or uncomfortable. Teachers should be much better supported in the classroom against unruly behaviour by students and by the school leadership against aggressive behaviour by parents.

15. **Teaching professionalism.** The General Teaching Council (GTC) should be abolished and recast as a far more rigorously professional body, upholding and championing the highest standards rather than acting as a trade union protecting teachers. The new GTC should be self-funded. If teachers are to have the status of other professions, such as

doctors and lawyers, they need to have a serious professional body at their head.

16. **More leadership by heads.** Heads should have more freedom to run their schools without constant oversight and reference back to governors and local authorities. But when heads show themselves to be unworthy of this autonomy because they are failing to give clear and visible leadership, governing bodies need to intervene, and either help the heads stand on their own feet, or promptly replace them if they are not going to make the grade. The aim of a good governing body is to appoint the head and to oversee the finances efficiently.

17. **School size.** All schools should have a human scale, where children are known and treated as unique individuals. Where schools exceed 600 in size, they should be broken down into smaller units, each with their own sub-head who will be able to personally know each pupil and set of parents. Students will benefit from an active sense of belonging to their house and to their school.

18. **Active parents and the community.** Successful schools actively involve parents and the community and will have thriving parents' assocations. This can take the form of ensuring that all parents sign a binding school contract. Schools should be free to open to the local community at all hours.

19. **ICT.** This could be used far more extensively than at present. But schools should be free to choose to use IT to help children to develop at their own pace, to work collaboratively, to undertake more original project research and work, and to adopt a problem-solving approach.

20. **The education 'establishment'.** The DCSF, QCDA, Ofqual, Ofsted, the TDA, SSAT, GTC and ISC should all undergo radical restructuring before 2015. They need to decentralise power, to facilitate rather than drive change and to work collaboratively rather than dictatorially. They should be far slimmer. They need to trust schools more and let creativity and individuality blossom, rather than be stifled by central blueprint.

2. WHY SCHOOLS?

The Dilemma

The word 'education' made its first appearance in 1531, according to the Oxford English Dictionary.[1] Education is a process of leading people out of a place of comparative ignorance into another place. It is a liberating experience, and implies an opening out, into a better and a more enriching world, of all the potentialities that make up a human being.

Governments, who across the world pay for the bulk of education, however, have a very different motive for it: they wish to train people for the national economy, socialise citizens to accept the values of society they expound and to prepare them, when necessary, to defend or assert the national interest. The 'top down' model from government can be at variance with the 'bottom up' model, of educating the whole human being. The former can be a narrowing experience, the latter is always a broadening one.

---

[1]   *Oxford English Dictionary,* Volume V, 1989.

A brief history of schools in three and a half pages

Schools have been provided not only by governments, but also by private companies, religious institutions, corporations and guilds. By the early nineteenth century, some schools existed for the poor, usually church schools. Grammar schools, which had existed for many years prior to 1800, lost some academic credibility in the early 19th century when they were discouraged from teaching modern languages and maths. Their plight helped boost public schools, which were patronised by the wealthy. The 1840s and 1850s saw an explosion in the number of public schools, including Brighton College in 1845 and Cheltenham Ladies College in 1853. The Liberal government of William Gladstone introduced the 1870 Education Act which sought to make education compulsory for all until the age of 12 and to make literacy and numeracy the right of every child.

The British performance in the Boer War of 1899-1902 nevertheless revealed the poor education and health of a vast proportion of the population, with many men rejected by the medical boards. These concerns, together with growing economic and military competition from the European powers, encouraged politicians to reform the education system. The 1902 Balfour Education Act tried to introduce more vigour into the system by putting voluntary and state education in the hands of Local Education Authorities.

The last hundred years in Britain have seen repeated attempts by governments to improve the quality of state education. The FIsher Act of 1918 raised the school leaving age to 14. The Butler Education Act of 1944 recast the mould of state education, establishing the three tier system of grammar schools for the most academically able, technical schools for those in the middle and secondary modern for the rest, with children's fate hanging on their performance in the 'eleven plus' test taken at the end of primary school. By 1964 there were 1,298 grammar schools, but the technical schools, designed to offer a practical education, never fully took off.[2] The performance of those regarded as educational 'failures' in the secondary moderns was predictably low.

After 1945 the Labour party made threatening noises about abolishing fee-paying schools for the wealthy. But when in power, Labour's nerve deserted it. Returned to office in 1964 under Harold Wilson, however, Labour's fire turned on grammar schools and 'direct grant' schools. In 1965, in the famous Crosland circular 10/65, the Government committed itself to the abolition of Butler's tripartite system in favour of all attending 'comprehensive' schools for children of all abilities. Local education authorities were given the task to reorganise their schools along comprehensive lines. Only eight of the 146 education authorities in England and Wales held out, including Kent, Buckinghamshire and Birmingham. Only 150 grammar schools were to remain by 1989, rising to 164 by 2009.[3] The elimination of almost 90% of the grammar school sector, a move designed to bolster equality of opportunity, in fact deepened educational apartheid in Britain. The abolition of 'direct grant' schools, which did not charge fees, led to many of them opting to become independent schools, thus denying another avenue for the young from non-privileged backgrounds.

---

[2] 'Grammar School Statistics', March 2009, House of Commons Library. http://www.parliament.uk/commons/lib/research/briefings/snsg-01398.pdf

[3] Ibid.

The Heath government of 1970-74 continued the drive towards comprehensivisation. The following Labour Government was too preoccupied by economic woes and had too little money to introduce significant educational change. The Prime Minister James Callaghan did launch the 'Great Education Debate' at Ruskin College in Oxford in 1976, although it failed to fulfil the expectations its grand title aroused.

For all Mrs Thatcher's reforming zeal as Prime Minister between 1979 and 1990, school organisation changed little under her. Her Government's 'assisted places scheme' did provide opportunities for children from poorer backgrounds, to have free or subsidised places in independent schools.

Concern with the low quality of much state school education, combined with a dislike of 'progressive' education and a distrust of the heavily unionised teaching profession, led to the 1988 Baker Education Reform Act. This was a curious mixture of free market principles and centrist prescription. The Act set up the National Curriculum, which dictated what schools were to teach: in contrast, the 1944 Act had made religious education the only compulsory subject.

When Labour was returned to power in 1997, their education policy was heavily informed by management consultant Michael Barber, who championed 'delivery, targets and measurements'. Under the more enlightened influence of Andrew Adonis from 2001, Labour became increasingly concerned to free up schools from central control, including the championing of 'academies', a move resisted by Chancellor Gordon Brown.

By the early 21st century, the factory school model was all but complete. Children arrived at nursery school at three or four and left school at the age of 16 or 18. The production line for children in school consisted of lessons punctuated by bells, which resulted in classes trooping off to different parts of the factory, from which they eventually emerged 11 or more years later with exam passes as the validation of their personal and school career. The factory was owned and operated under the strict top-down instructions of government, who decreed everything that went on.

It is the apogee of Fordism gone mad.[4]

What are schools doing well?

Not all schools are bad.

Many children are happy and successful, and leave with excellent qualifications. The 2009 OECD report, *Doing better for children,* praised spending levels in Britain per child, finding them to be higher than the OECD average, and it placed Britain fourth for its quality of school life.[5]

The education establishment also points to the high exam results. Today, pass rates and top grades are higher at A-Levels and GCSEs and their Scottish and Northern Irish equivalents, than ever.

Never before had two successive prime ministers, Tony Blair and Gordon Brown, given education such a high personal priority, nor invested so much of their personal time in it (nor had the twentieth century seen two successive prime ministers with children of nursery school age). Rarely, if ever, had there been a

---

[4]   'The use in manufacturing industry of the methods pioneered by Henry Ford esp. Large-scale mechanized mass production.' *Shorter Oxford English Dictionary* , Oxford University Press, 2007):

[5]   OECD, *Doing better for children,* 2009.

secretary of state with the responsibility for schools with the same political weight of Ed Balls, Gordon Brown's closest adviser, as he had been for the 15 years before 2010.

But the area of greatest success is the independent sector. British independent schools are rated to be the best out of the 32 countries surveyed in a 2002 OECD report.[6]

What are schools doing less well?
So with greater investment in schools, a better pupil-teacher ratio, and a higher level of exam results than ever before in British history, why the concern?

School failings: the employers' perspective
The CBI, Institute of Directors (IoD) and individual employers have repeatedly complained about the standards of literacy, numeracy, personal and social skills from school leavers. For example, Richard Lambert, the CBI's Director General, said in August 2009 that 'school leavers must be armed with basic skills otherwise they will struggle throughout their career',[7] and in January 2010 said we should be 'ashamed' of school results and the failure to do more for poorer children.[8] Over 50% of employers reported, in mid-2009, that they were unhappy in particular with school leavers' numeracy and literacy rates.[9]

The CBI wants more children to be taught maths and science (estimates suggest that there will be a requirement for two million

---

6   OECD, *Education at a glance*, 2002.

7   'CBI reaction to Ofsted report on diplomas', CBI website, 17 August 2009.

8   *The Guardian*, 1 January 2010.

9   'CBI praises students on the years GCSE results', CBI website, 27 August 2009.

science-related jobs by 2015).[10] There are critical shortages of those suitable for engineering. In contrast to France, where two-thirds of students continue to study maths after the age of 16, in England the figure is only 9%.[11] One CBI survey found that 50% of employers complained that young people were inarticulate, unable to communicate concisely or interpret written instructions. Sir Terence Leahy, CEO of Tesco, has attacked British educational standards as 'woefully low'.[12] He said that five million adults were functionally illiterate and 17 million could not add up properly. Michael Rake, chairman of British Telecom, castigated the quality of GCSEs and A-Levels, which he said should be scrapped: 'what we want are people who are employable, people who have practical skills.'[13] Sir Christopher Gent, chairman of GlaxoSmithKline, argues similarly: 'the transformation of the A-Level in to a "one size fits all" system combined with the drive to promote equivalence between the vocational and academic qualifications has failed to meet the needs of the nation... The consequent decline in the nation's scientific base is now a major problem for business.'[14] A KPMG study estimated that the British

---

[10] 'CBI applauds this year's A-level students', CBI website, 20 August 2009.

[11] 'Britain needs more people coming out of school, college and university with maths as part of their skills armoury', CBI website, 20 August 2009. See also Harriet Sergeant, 'Schools are churning out the unemployable,' *The Sunday Times,* 21 February 2010.

[12] 'Tesco's Sir Terry Leahy attacks government education record', *The Daily Telegraph*, 13 October 2009.

[13] 'GCSEs and A-Levels should be scrapped says BT chairman', *The Daily Telegraph*, 14 October 2009.

[14] Sir Christopher Gent, 'Remarks to Marlborough and Wellington Colleges', RSA Conference on the IB, 12 October 2009.

economy loses £2.4 billion a year because its citizens have a poor grasp of maths and science.[15]

And this failure to educate children has drastic consequences for the employment prospects of the least fortunate: in 2009, there were 928,000 18-24 year olds who were NEETs (Not in Employment, Education or Training), 17.2% of the total.[16] And a 2009 OECD report worryingly found that 10% of 15-19 year olds were NEETs, which is significantly above the OECD average.[17]

School failure: the Universities' perspective
Universities, too, are becoming ever-more dissatisfied with the 'products' they are receiving from schools. Part of the problem is that although over three-quarters of students who take A-Levels go on to university, universities have played little part in framing the exams.[18] Many of the top universities find that A-Levels fail to discriminate sufficiently between the intellectually able and the merely well-drilled, and with 26.7% of papers achieving 'A' grades in 2009, there are simply too many awarded the top grade for the places available.[19] Members of the 'Russell Group', which represents the top 20 universities in terms of research grants and funding, thus ask prospective law students to sit the National Admissions Test for Law. Universities that run medicine, dentistry

---

[15]   KPMG, *Innumerate school children cost the tax payer up to £2.4bn a year*, 2009.

[16]   'Number of Neets reaches new high as recession bites', *The Daily Telegraph*, 18 August 2009.

[17]   OECD, *Doing better for children*, 2009.

[18]   Dale Bassett et al, *A New Level*, Reform, 2009.

[19]   John O'Leary, 'Calls for tougher marking after yet another A-grade bonanza', *The Independent*, 21 August 2009.

and veterinary courses demand that students sit preliminary exams. Oxford runs admissions tests for Politics, Philosophy and Economics aspirants, and also in History and English. Cambridge asks students to sit admissions tests in Modern and Medieval Languages, Computer Science, Natural Sciences, Engineering, Economics and Mathematics.[20] It also lists 20 A-Level subjects which it considers only to be suitable as a third or fourth grade, even though they accrue the same number of UCAS points as more academic A-Levels.[21]

Geoff Parks, director of admissions at Cambridge has frequently voiced his concerns about the deficiencies of A-Levels and GCSEs to prepare students for, or even to test, genuine intellectual rigour and ability. He dismissed GCSEs as a 'treadmill' that does not allow for 'originality'.[22]

School failure: unhappy children
Schools should help to produce young men and young women who are self-reliant, not dependent on alcohol or drugs, and capable of leading happy and meaningful lives. But in March 2009, it was reported that 74% of young people thought that the education system needed to change to meet their needs better.[23] The UK has been rated as a poor place for children to grow up in, being ranked bottom out of the 22 countries

---

[20] John O'Leary, *The Times Good University Guide 2009*, 2008.

[21] Ibid. See also Anna Fazackerley and Julian Chant, *The Hard Truth about 'soft' subjects*, Policy Exchange, December 2008.

[22] 'Bright pupils favour new alternatives to the GCSE treadmill', *The Times*, 25 August 2009.

[23] Edge website, 'Young people's attitudes to the education system', 21 January 2009.

investigated. It was fourth worst for 'educational well-being', and worst for 'family and peer relationships', 'behaviours and risk', and 'subjective well-being'.[24] The 2009 OECD report found only 36% of children 'liked' school, and that British children were twice as likely to be drunk before the age of 15 than children in any other OECD country.[25] Another survey ranked Britain 24th for child well-being and 22nd on schooling. Only Latvia, Lithuania, Bulgaria, Malta and Romania did worse.[26]

School failure: low education standards
Standards in state schools have not risen in aggregate. True, exam results have been better, but this is because of 'grade inflation', not because the students are necessarily any better. In 2000, the PISA analysis showed that Britain came 8th for maths, 4th for science and 7th in reading and literacy. By 2006 it had fallen to 24th, 14th and 17th respectively.[27] In 2009, the number of pupils leaving primary school achieving a 'level 5' score in English and Science fell for the second successive year, leading to questions about whether the Government's literacy and numeracy strategy for primary schools has been the success that has been claimed for it.[28]

---

[24]   UNICEF, *Child Poverty in Perspective: An overview of Child Well-being in Rich Countries*, 2007.

[25]   OECD, *Doing better for children*, 2009.

[26]   York University, *Child Wellbeing and Child Poverty*, 2009.

[27]   PISA, *2006: Science Competencies for Tomorrow's World*, 2007.

[28]   ONS, *Education and Training Statistics for the United Kingdom: 2009*, 2009.

School failure: continuing 'education apartheid'

The dream of the great education reform politicians – including Gladstone, Balfour, Fisher and Butler – was to improve opportunities for all children regardless of social background. The decision by politicians of both main parties to have a universal comprehensive system and abolish grammar and direct grant schools would, it was hoped, reverse the trend towards greater social mobility, which has increased still further in the last ten years.

But it has not. Pupils in advantaged areas are now six times more likely to go to university, while in the poorest constituencies, less than 1 in 10 young people go on to higher education.[29] In 2008, 23,000 students secured three 'A' grades at A-Level, but only 189 of them were receiving free school meals (FSM), a core indicator of relative poverty.[30] Eton College alone achieved a quarter more clutches of 3 'A' grades than the entire number on FSMs, who constitute 15% of the pupils in British schools. A Sutton Trust Report in 2009 found that 'far from raising opportunities for all irrespective of background, the education system has served to perpetuate inequalities'.[31] A Conservative Party study found that independent school pupils are four times more likely to achieve three A grades at A-Level, up from 3.5 times more likely ten years ago.[32]

---

[29] HEFCE, *Young participation in higher education,* 2005.

[30] House of Commons written answers for 26 November 2008, *Hansard,* 26 November 2009, col. 1857w.

[31] Sutton Trust, *Social Mobility and Education,* June 2008.

[32] Conservative Party press release, 'Widening education gap between the many and the few' 21 February 2010.

The Education 'Establishment'

For schools, this is made up of a variety of bodies, including at the apex the school's department in Whitehall, currently called the Department for Children, Schools and Families (DCSF). Below this is the Qualifications and Curriculum Authority (QCA), set up in 1997, and shortly to become the Qualifications and Curriculum Development Agency (QCDA). The aim of this body is to oversee the curriculum, improve and deliver assessment, and to review and reform qualifications. 'Ofqual' is the independent qualifications regulator, initially set up in 2008 but not formalised until April 2010. 'Ofsted' is the body that oversees inspections, set up in 1992, under the leadership of Her Majesty's Chief Inspector. The Teaching Development Agency (TDA) was set up as the Teaching Training Agency in 1994 and is responsible for the initial and in-service training of teachers and other support staff. The National College of School Leadership was set up in 1998 to train and develop heads and other school leaders. The General Teaching Council (GTC) is the professional body for teaching in England, whose task is to improve standards for teaching and learning and was also set up in 1998. Finally, there is the Specialist Schools and Academies Trust (SSAT), set up in 1997.

The Centre for Policy Studies has argued cogently for many of these bodies to be heavily pruned or swept away.[33] Chris Woodhead, the former chief inspector, describes them as 'the Blob', and says that if the Conservatives win in 2010 they will have a major task in taking on the education establishment and winning.[34]

---

[33] See for example, Tom Burkard and Sam Talbot Rice, *School Quangos: An agenda for abolition and reform*, Centre for Policy Studies, 2009.

[34] *Standpoint*, Michael Gove and Chris Woodhead in interview, January/February 2010.

These bodies are full of many hard working and highly professional individuals, who have tried to improve educational standards and opportunities for students.

They are, however, all the products of a 'top-down', centrist approach. All of them, including the Whitehall department, need radical rethinking if schools are to be independent.

Education as a unique service

Archon Fung of Harvard University has argued for 'accountable autonomy' for schools (and police).[35] He argues for high degrees of independence to be given to schools and parents, but within the context of clear accountability and certain minimum national standards. The job of government, he says, is not to run schools or to impose their own diktats, but to enable localities to create their own schools within this broad framework.

This approach has much to commend it. It inspires the thinking behind this report. For, after one hundred years of ever more centralised factory schools, it is time to give schools far greater independence.

What could independence mean?

In the last ten years, a consensus has emerged between both major political parties that schools do not need to continue to be subjected to the same high degrees of stifling central control, and that they would benefit from greater degrees of freedom. Labour and the Conservatives disagree on the extent

---

[35] Archon Fung, "Accountable Autonomy: Toward Empowered Deliberation in Chicago schools and policing", *Politics and Society,* Vol. 29, March 2001. See also Archon Fung, *Empowered Participation: Reinventing Urban Democracy,* Princeton University Press, 2006.

of that independence, and within Labour, divisions have also been pronounced. The Brownites repeatedly stopped Blair making schools even freer, especially in 2005 and 2006.

What are the range of freedoms that schools could have?

- Total legal freedom to act as an independent company within the law.
- Freedom to make a profit and to raise their own capital.
- Freedom to select their own pupils without any central direction.
- Freedom to spend their money entirely as they wish.
- Freedom to decide the hours that teachers should work.
- Freedom to appoint and dismiss teachers and support staff and decide on the ratios of each.
- Freedom to choose their own curriculum and their own examination system.
- Freedom to punish and exclude pupils without appeal or reference to external bodies.
- Freedom to decide on the length and organisation of the school day and the length and timing of holidays.

True financial independence for schools is also a prerequisite. This could be achieved by basing their income on their ability to attract parents and pupils, not on the discretion of the funding authorities. To achieve this, schools should be funded directly by central government on a standard formula based on pupil numbers, with the money being paid into the schools' bank accounts. The formula should be simple enough for any interested party – parent or commentator – to calculate the amount payable using a pencil and paper. It must not be clothed in secrecy or be too complex for anyone to understand (as state school funding is today).

Schools should be delegated 100% of the funding necessary for the provision of education. They would then be free to buy the support services they needed from any organisation they saw fit. In particular, they should be free to buy back services from their local authority, if they wished, or any other local authority, either in the adjacent area or further afield. They could also choose to buy the services from the private sector instead. Local authorities would have no monopoly of service provision in their areas.

3. LEARNING AND TEACHING

The Dilemma

If schools are left to teach whatever they wish, too little ground may be covered, the pace may be too slow, material may be repeated as children move from school to school, and that the curriculum may be determined too much by and in the interests of the teachers rather than the learners. The curriculum may thus be repetitive, incoherent and incomplete. The children may be indoctrinated into closed ideologies and belief systems.

But if the state dictates exactly what is to be taught and learned, it rides roughshod over the particular interests and specialisms of each local school and locality. The material and pace will be inappropriate for some, and the professionalism and judgement of teachers will be marginalised. What must be found is a dynamic balance between the polar opposites of total school freedom and crushing central direction, with the balance tipped firmly towards the former.

A 'free' curriculum

The 1902 Balfour Education Act handed over the content of the curriculum entirely to teachers. Similarly, the 1944 Act made no requirement for the curriculum other than specifying that religious education be taught as a compulsory subject. In practice, schools taught a common curriculum of English, Maths, Science, modern languages, history and geography, with the more academic state schools, and independent schools, continuing to have a heavy emphasis on the teaching of classics. Callaghan's 1976 speech was a stage in the move away from the free curriculum. But it was with the arrival of the Conservatives in 1979 that central control over the curriculum greatly increased.

The factory curriculum

The 1988 National Curriculum took the content of education out of the hands of professionals and placed it squarely in the hands of government. The working parties that were set up to establish programmes of study and attainment targets contained surprisingly few teachers and professionals in a process that was to create one of the world's most rigorous and prescribed curriculums.[1]

Teachers could no longer teach what they wanted; the curriculum was policed by the National Curriculum Council (NCC) set up in 1988, whose brief was to oversee the subject-based National Curriculum, deciding the knowledge, understanding and skills to be taught in each subject. By 1989, huge ring-binders were landing on teachers' desks outlining the new curriculum, and by the early 2000s, some teachers were wading through as many as 6,000 pages of curriculum a year.[2]

---

[1]   Stephen Ward and Christine Eden, *Key issues in education policy*, Sage Publications, 2009.

[2]   David Coulby and Leslie Bash, *Contradiction and Conflict: The 1988 Education Reform Act in action*, Cassell, 1991. 'Teachers buried in 6000 pages of government bureaucracy', *The Daily Telegraph*, 21 December 2008.

The National Curriculum was not without its benefits: all children, regardless of their school or the location of their home could be guaranteed to cover core content in each subject in a way that was at best developmental rather than random. It redressed some of the less desirable 'child-centred' innovations made following the Plowden Report. Much of the prescribed material was appropriate and stimulating, and it gave content to teachers who were either lacking in the confidence or energy to devise their own. But the centrally imposed curriculum had several disadvantages:

De-professionalisation
It de-professionalised teachers, because they were being told exactly what to teach and the pace at which they were to teach it, rather than exercising their own judgement, tastes and specialism. Being a professional entails the exercise of judgement and discretion, not carrying out the instructions of others. Recently, Chris Woodhead, the former Chief-Inspector of Schools, wrote that 'teaching is no longer a profession. By definition, professionals are expected to determine their own beliefs and practice. This is no longer the case in England'.[3]

'Dumbs down' teaching
A rigid curriculum made teaching less attractive to the intellectually most able graduates. If the teacher is not able to exercise his or her judgement, but is merely trotting out material determined elsewhere, the best are less likely to want to teach. The idea grew that school teaching was not a career for those with 'original minds'.

---

[3] Politeia, *Teachers Matter: Recruitment, Employment and Retention at home and abroad*, July 2009.

Artificially separates subjects

It encourages 'silo' thinking, by determining that subjects such as maths, biology, chemistry, English language, modern languages, history and geography be taught separately. But no subject is entirely discrete. They are, like the world they describe, inextricably connected. Interconnections between subjects need to be highlighted to students for a full understanding of the world; chemistry cannot be understood without biology, physics without maths, science without history, geography without chemistry and so on. In the words of the novelist Susan Hill, 'we have lost sight of the whole joy and purpose of education'.[4] Ultimately, subjects become dry and meaningless if not related to other disciplines and to the real world.

Narrow vision of education

The National Curriculum has been imposed at the expense of a broader vision of educating the whole child. But the human being, and the achievement of the human race, depends upon far more than measurable intellectual processing skills. In 1983 Howard Gardner of Harvard University developed his model of 'multiple intelligences', of seven different intelligences (later expanded to eight).[5] While this is still controversial, it is surely common sense to recognise that students – and indeed all individuals – do have a variety of different intelligences; and that education should be directed towards drawing these out, rather than focusing exclusively on academic intelligence.

---

[4]   Susan Hill, 'Must Try Harder', *Standpoint*, September 2009.

[5]   Howard Gardner, *Frames of Mind: the theory of multiple intelligences*, Basic Books, 1983.

Indeed, a notable characteristic of successful independent schools is that they offer extensive programmes catering for these intelligences as part of their 'extra-curricular' or 'co-curricular' programmes, with culture, sport, community service and leadership training all stressed. Wellington College has developed its own 'octagon model', where the mission is to identify, nurture and develop all eight intelligences or aptitudes which lie within each child. These are made up of four sets of pairs: the logical and linguistic, the creative and physical, the spiritual and moral, and the personal and social aptitudes.

With less time in a school day, and fewer teachers per student, state schools have had less opportunity to offer this kind of education. In December 2009 the Sutton Trust announced that it was launching an experiment into a ten hour day to include time for wider enrichment.[6] The Sutton Trust is drawing inspiration from the Knowledge is Power Programme (KIPP) in the US, which utilises longer school days to offer a broader vision of education.[7] The 2009 Nuffield Review of 14-19 education and training called for 'The re-assertion of a broader vision of education – in which there is a profound respect for the whole person (not just the narrowly conceived 'intellectual excellence' or 'skills for economic prosperity').[8]

---

[6] 'New report reveals stark education gaps beyond the classroom'. http://www.suttontrust.com/news.asp#a068

[7] 'Factory Schools don't give real education', *The Times*, 22 December 2009.

[8] Richard Pring et al, *Nuffield review of 14-19 Education and Training, England and Wales*, Nuffield Foundation, 2009.

Superficial content

Even within the National Curriculum, many young people are still being denied genuine depth of curriculum knowledge. Historian Dominic Sandbrook has, for example, complained that history students at university are profoundly lacking in knowledge of much of the sweep of history, while topics such as Nazi Germany or the US Civil Rights Movement are studied in great and repetitive depth.[9] Historian David Starkey also decried the low emphasis on content in British schools: in 2009 he said 'the notion that you need to hold knowledge in your head seems to have been forgotten... It's not good enough to say you can look things up on the web. You can produce connections only if you know facts.'[10] Likewise Martin Stephen, High Master of St Paul's School in London, has castigated the failure of GCSEs: 'They are simply pap, they are baby food, they are examination rusks in too many subjects, and they do not stretch and challenge the most able'.[11]

Originality squeezed

A centrally imposed curriculum, by its very nature, is unable to place sufficient emphasis on thinking and originality. In place of creativity, it requires too much on passive listening. Today the challenge is of information overload: young people need to be able to cope with a mass of information, to process it, and to present arguments based upon it while also making independent intellectual moral judgments.

---

[9]   'Once upon a time there was a subject called history', *The Daily Telegraph*, 14 September 2009.

[10]   'School producing a generation of illiterates, says David Starkey', *The Times*, 1 May 2009.

[11]   'Top private school dumps 'too easy' GCSEs', *The Guardian*, 4 March 2009.

Creativity is being squeezed out of the classroom. What a teacher or adult tells a child will always be the property of that teacher or that adult: what a child discovers for themselves will always be owned by that child. Creativity does not need to be 'taught' as it is innate, but it needs time to draw it out. Schools instead tend to squeeze the creativity out of children by failing to nurture individuality, creative responses and culture, and by allowing a climate in which young people are afraid to make mistakes or be seen to express themselves in ways that invite ridicule from their peers.[12]

A dilemma to be resolved

The Conservatives are advocating that schools should be free to choose their own curriculum; academies would be able virtually to ignore the National Curriculum. So far, so good.

But, at the same time, the Conservatives are caught in the dilemma outlined at the beginning of this chapter. They want to give schools and teachers freedom but they also have a powerful wish to dictate what children are taught. In his speech to the Royal Society of Arts in June 2009, Shadow Education Secretary Michael Gove talked of the 'neglected giants' of science and history, was critical of subjects such as media studies and citizenship, and said:[13]

> '[The] British people's common sense inclines them towards schools in which the principal activity is teaching and learning, the principal goal is academic

---

[12] Take for example Ken Robinson's speech to the RSA in June 2008: http://www.thersa.org/events/vision/vision-videos/sir-ken-robinson

[13] Michael Gove, 'What is Education For?', Speech to the RSA, 29 June 2009.

attainment, and the principal guiding every action is the wider spread of excellence, the initiation of new generations into the amazing achievements of humankind. Because that is what education is for.'

The way out of the dilemma

It is possible to combine greater decentralisation and trust for professionals with raising attainment and a greater academic emphasis on the teaching of academic subjects. This is to let schools follow validated programmes like the International Baccalaureate (IB), and to prescribe minimum levels of achievement that students should have at the end of each of the five key stages.

The International Baccalaureate Organisation (IBO) runs three separate programmes, the Diploma Programme for 16 to 19 year olds, the 'Middle Year Programme' (MYP) for 11 to 16 year olds, and the 'Primary Years Programme' (PYP) for 3 to 11 year olds. The IB 'learner profile', which runs through all the programmes, aims to develop 'internationally minded' people, who amongst other attributes, are enquirers with their natural curiosity developed, are active and critical thinkers can express themselves confidently and in more than one language, are highly principled and honest, are open-minded, risk-taking and reflective. The IB offers genuine intellectual depth but also emphasises the 'interconnectedness' of academic disciplines, with its 'theory of knowledge' paper in the diploma programme. The IB is not perfect – its aspirations do not always match the reality, and it can be burdensome bureaucratically[14] – but it is the most complete system currently available in the world.

---

[14] See for example Anthony Seldon, *A Newcomer's Critique of the IB*, Seville Heads' conference, October 2008.

Another example of a new – and apparently successful – approach is the Harkness method where students take responsibility for their own learning. Harkness tables were introduced first at Phillips Academy in the US and involve students sitting at oval tables witht he teacher giding learngin rather than lecturing. This approach was intorduced successfully at Wellington College in 2008.

Some conclusions on learning and teaching

Diversity and experimentation in learning and teaching, in examination and curricula, should all be welcomed in British state schools (just as they are in British independent schools). There will be failures. But we should trust parents to choose the best school for their child from as wide a range of schools as possible.

4. SCHOOL ETHOS AND DISCIPLINE

The Dilemma

The educational establishment, including Christine Gilbert, Her Majesty's Chief Inspector of Schools, does not believe that bad behaviour in the classroom continues to be a significant problem. Alan Steer, who was charged by the Government to investigate behaviour in schools, concluded that 'standards are high in the large majority of schools'.[1] Following Steer's final report, the DCSF believes that 'the majority of schools have good or outstanding behaviour'.[2]

But 'feeling unsafe in the classroom' is the number one reason why undergraduates (18%) and professionals (20%) do not want to become teachers.[3] A Teachernet survey published in June found that 49% of teachers (of 414 surveyed) had been threatened with violence, 40% had been physically attacked,

---

[1] Letter from Sir Alan Steer to Ed Balls, 6 February 2009.

[2] 'Behaviour challenge set for secondary schools', DCSF, 30 September 2009.

[3] Sam Freedman et al, *More Good Teachers*, Policy Exchange, 2008.

95% had been verbally abused in some way, 87% had no confidence in searching a pupil for a weapon, 46% felt confident in using reasonable force to stop a pupil harming themselves or others, and 25% had been falsely accused of violence at some point.[4] In 2008 there were 83,000 exclusions due to physical violence and 94,740 for verbal abuse.[5] There were 8,310 permanent exclusions. Getting discipline 'right' clearly matters: Kathy August, of Manchester Academy on Moss Side, which has seen a spectacular improvement in academic results in the last decade, has said that the success can be put down to 'a zero tolerance attitude to poor behaviour'.[6]

But discipline is a notoriously difficult subject. At one end of the scale are teachers (sometimes entire schools) which appear to be very lax but where learning and relationships are excellent; while at the other end are teachers and schools who run harsh discipline regimes, and where the children react against them, and where bad relationships and poor discipline predominate. It should be obvious, therefore, that a single policy to improve discipline cannot be imposed on all schools from the centre.

A way out of the dilemma
Again, schools must be free to find out what works best for each individual school. One model does not fit all. Everything depends upon the style of the head, the ethos of the school,

---

[4] 'More Action at local level needed to tackle widespread violence and disruption in schools', Teachers Support Network Survey, June 2009.

[5] DCSF, *Permanent and fixed period exclusions from schools and exclusion appeals in England, 2007/08,* 2009.

[6] 'Top marks for Manchester Academy – addressing the class divide', *The Guardian,* 1 January 2010.

and the strategies employed by the individual teachers. That said, the following are common characteristics of successful learning environments:

Good relationships
These are essential within a school, between adults and students, and students with other students. Where relationships are positive, children want to learn, want to behave well and want to contribute. There is not a good school in the world which does not enjoy positive relationships.

Formal standards are necessary
There should be a regulation school uniform which should be worn with pride: students and parents should respect the school and should abide by the rulings that the school gives: punctuality and attendance are essential for the smooth running of the school. Schools are not social clubs, and work best with a degree of formality.

'Positive psychology' should underpin all a school does
When president of the American Psychological Association, Professor Martin Seligman asked the following question: why so much of psychology was concerned with abnormality and mental illness, rather than also examining the ingredients of a meaningful, full and happy life? Out of this questioning was born positive psychology, an approach that has been shown to be effective.

Some of its principal features are: emphasising genuinely positive achievement by children; students prioritising doing good to others above feeling good themselves; finding and highlighting strengths rather than weaknesses; stressing the need for physical health including regular exercise, good diet and sufficient sleep; emphasising the importance of gratitude and appreciation; and insisting upon high, but also realistic, expectations of students at all times.

This body of work has been discredited in Britain by its flawed introduction in the form of Social And Emotional Learning (SEAL) lessons. These have been rightly attacked from a number of quarters.[7] But the failure of SEAL should not undermine the case for positive psychology, properly taught, in schools. Above all, positive psychology should not take valuable lesson time away from academic subjects: rather it should inform the whole ethos of the school, for students, teachers and parents to benefit.

Values

Positive values are essential for the underpinning of all good learning environments. While most schools are no longer expressly religious, some state schools have been remarkably successful in highlighting values throughout the school like respect, responsibility and tolerance.[8] Harry Brighouse, the academic and author, has also argued that secular pupils will flourish in religious schools in part because of their emphasis on good values and ethics. Successful charter schools in the US, such as the Excel academy in East Boston, stress positive values such as 'be respectful' throughout their entire school.[9]

---

[7]   See for example, Carol Craig, *The curious case of the tail wagging the dog*, Centre for Confidence and Wellbeing, 2009.

[8]   See Neil Hawkes and Linda Heppenstall, *Living Values – one primary school's way of encouraging a values-based education*, Royal College of Psychology, 2002. Neil Hawkes was head of West Kidlington Primary and Nursery School in Oxfordshire during the 1990s where he achieved enormous success by initiating a strong value-based programme.

[9]   *The Times Educational Supplement*, 11 February 2009.

Service
Fundamental to any successful school is children taking responsibility, not only for their own learning but also for their behaviour and their lives. Helping others should thus be a core part of every school. The young should be able to learn the importance and joy of caring for others.[10]

All students should therefore be encouraged to spend a year engaged in 'national community service' after they leave school.[11] Programmes could be made up of outdoor adventure and training by the military, community service projects, and teaching about leadership, teamwork and self reliance.[12]

Outdoor experience and physical challenge
All children should have experience of outdoor activity. One practical way for many young people to experience outdoor activity is through schemes such as the Duke of Edinburgh awards and 'Combined Cadet Forces' (CCF). All schools should be encouraged to run CCF programmes for students aged between 14 and 16, to teach them about teamwork, self reliance and leadership.[13]

---

[10] A recent report from Demos rightly stressed the importance of community service, which is believed 'would instil values of active citizenship from primary school age onwards.' See Sonia Sodha and Dan Leighton, *Service Nation,* Demos, 2009.

[11] This could be compulsory. Germany, Israel and Norway all have compulsory national service programmes.

[12] Anthony Seldon, *Trust: How we lost it and How to Get it Back,* Biteback, 2009.

[13] An excellent book on outdoor education is Colin Mortlock's, *The Adventure Alternative,* Cicerone Press, 1984.

Self-discipline not discipline

The aim in every good school is for students to behave well from inner wish rather than external fear of punishment. A young person with self-discipline and a properly developed sense of responsibility will be a good learner and a good citizen.

Schools do not give students nearly enough responsibility. It is extraordinary what even 'problem' pupils will achieve if trusted with responsibility. Many schools patronise pupils by not giving them trust. 'Student voice' is growing in schools, and rightly, but it needs to be centred on students taking their responsibilities and duties seriously, not demanding 'rights'.

Active thinking and philosophy

All students should be taught about thinking, and philosophy, even in primary school. Even young children should not be patronised, and be kept away from being made to think about philosophy. 'Philosophy 4 Children' is a movement which aims to teach reasoning methods to children.

Some conclusions on school discipline and ethos

There are clearly many ways in which school discipline and ethos can be improved. Equally, it is clear that it should be the responsibility of each individual school to decide how to develop the ethos and discipline policy which is right for that school.

5. ASSESSING STUDENTS AND SCHOOLS

Dilemma

The ideal is for schools to be free standing institutions, run with a high degree of autonomy, and with pupil assessment being designed to facilitate learning. But if schools are left unchecked and uninspected, there is no guarantee that some may not let down their students with shoddy standards and poor teaching. If pupils are not assessed regularly, there is no way of knowing how much they are learning, and how effective their teachers are.

But schools which are over-monitored and over-inspected experience fear and resentment. And if exams and league tables are too predominant – as they are in Britain today – the assessment determines the curriculum and the whole school's *raison d'être*, rather than the way round.

Assessing pupils

Since the 1990s, the principal monitor of the effectiveness of schools has become league tables. Like almost everything else connected with British education, league tables have desirable and undesirable features, but the latter are now predominant. League tables were initially crude and took no account of the ability or background of the intake of the pupils. More sophisticated league tables, measuring 'value-added' were subsequently introduced. These aim to assess the contribution made by the school to students' academic improvement, taking account of their academic achievement on joining the school.

The function of exams
Exams have six purposes:

- To indicate the different levels of the student's understanding in a subject.
- To give universities information on a student.
- To show future employers the level of ability reached by potential employees in different subjects.
- To provide a focal point and stimulus for a student, and a means of self evaluation.
- To offer a method of evaluating and comparing the ability of different teachers, sets and schools in the quality of the effectiveness of their exam preparation.
- To provide a focus for the curriculum.

Exams were first introduced into England at Cambridge University in 1792. A-Levels and O-Levels were both introduced in 1951. In 1986, O-Levels were replaced by GCSEs. With the National Curriculum from 1988 came tests at the end of the various Key stages: KS1 at age 7, KS2 at 11, KS3 at 14, and KS4 at 16 (GCSEs) making British children among the most examined in the world. The GCSE had an important change in emphasis with greater weight than O-levels placed on skills rather than content.

From the time they were introduced, the marking of GCSEs changed from a system based on 'norm-referencing' where a fixed percentage of candidates got the top grade (around 10%), and the next percentage received the second grade and so on, to a system of 'criterion referencing' where examiners were told to look for certain levels of attainment, which would then result in the award of a certain grade. The same shift from norm to criterion marking had earlier taken place for A-Level in 1984. Theoretically this now meant that 100% of candidates could achieve A grades in A-Levels and GCSEs. The justification for the shift was that teachers would positively reward merit and that teachers would be encouraged to help students reach certain standards with greater transparency and fairness in marking.

Ten years ago, 'Curriculum 2000' reformed A-levels and introduced AS-levels in the lower sixth (Year 12) and A2 exams at the end of the upper sixth (Year 13), breaking down each of these two exams further into a series of modules to be taken separately, and which could be retaken several times. This change to a modular structure marked the decisive point when rote-learning and instruction took over from genuine and active learning and teaching.

Exams and the curriculum are overseen in Britain by the Qualifications and Curriculum Authority (QCA), set up in 1997, to become the QCDA in 2010. The QCA has for much of its brief history been an inward-looking body which has been more concerned to defend the *status quo* than keep abreast with the best educational practice. Ofqual has now been set up to try to ensure that qualifications are independent of government, and to improve trust in the system. But it is unlikely to achieve its aspirations. Simon Lebus, chief executive of Cambridge Assessments, believes, despite Ofqual, that government will continue to try to exert control over the curriculum. Alison Wolf is another who believes that government will continue to try to interfere in qualifications. As Patrick Watson summarises that: 'the establishment of Ofqual was supposed to signal a move back to independent quality assurance, with light regulation, but it appears too close to government and few insiders believe that it will make much difference.[1]

Problems with factory assessment
There are many problems with this style of assessment.

Grade inflation
In 1984, the year that criterion marking was introduced, 38% of A-Level papers received an A to C grade, in 2009, 73.9% of A-Level papers were awarded an A to C grade.[2] Does this mean that sixth formers are now twice as intelligent as they were 20 years ago? Mike Cresswell, director general of AQA, one of the examination boards, certainly thinks that students are better: 'today's A-Level candidates, I think – work harder than I ever did'.[3] Others disagree. A recent report, *Straight As?*, sought to explain grade inflation by polling teachers.[4] None thought the increase in grades was due to students being more able: 4% said better quality of teaching was the reason, 20% thought re-sits were responsible, and 29% thought that student knowledge of what examiners were looking for was the key factor. The report cited various anonymous teachers all of whom have the ring of authenticity. A head of Sixth Form from Yorkshire said:

---

[1] Patrick Watson, *Central Control and Intervention over Curriculum*, 30 October 2009.

[2] Durham University, *Education Briefing Book 2008*, 2008.

[3] 'Calls for tougher marking after yet another A-grade bonanza', *The Independent*, 21 August 2009.

[4] Anastasia de Waal, *Straight A's?*, Civitas, 2009. The following quotations come from this report.

'There is a real problem with re-sits and the re-sit culture – I would abolish them. Students are revising for re-sits when they should be focusing on the current course.'

A head of Sixth Form in London said: 'it's not good from the point of education, its repeating ad nauseam', while a head of Sixth Form from the south east said 'it's total nonsense how things have improved'. In 2000, 230,000 students took A-Levels requiring 2.17 million papers: by 2008, only a small percentage more, 257,000 students, sat A-Levels, but took well over double the number of papers.[5]

The *status quo,* however, has powerful supporters. Grade inflation benefits students, teachers, schools and local education authorities. All of them are able to claim that they are doing better.

But as with money inflation, hidden dangers lurk. A report by Durham University found that despite a steady rise in A-Level grades, standards remained relatively stable. Their conclusion is clear:[6]

> 'CEM (Curriculum Evaluation and Management Centre of Durham University) data shows that candidates of comparable ability are being awarded higher grades each year, both at A-level – where the trend has been consistent and substantial since 1988 – and at GCSE, where the

---

[5]   Dale Bassett, Thomas Cawston, Laurie Thraves, Elizabeth Truss, *A New Level,* Reform, 2009.

[6]   Durham University, *Education Briefing Book 2008,* 2008.

change seems a little smaller and more intermittent. From 1988 to 2007, achievement levels at A-level have risen by an average of just over 2 grades in each subject considered in the research. Exceptionally, from 1988 the rise appears to be over 3.5 grades for mathematics.'

Teaching to the test

The more precise and prescriptive the advice in marking schemes to examiners, the more that exam questions have been broken down into small sections with individual marks, the greater the possibilities of retaking exams, and the more forensically marking schemes are studied in classes, the more schools have come to teach, not academic subjects, but exam techniques. Brave is the teacher who teaches material 'not on the syllabus', or who spends time teaching topics and approaches which are not strictly specified. Parents, students, and heads demand to know why class time has been used 'indulgently'. Creativity and individuality is squeezed out of teaching, and the role of the teacher becomes that of a technician guiding students along a precise and well-designed response to what is required by the marking scheme. Liberal education is sacrificed to instruction, freedom of expression to learning the right answer, and genuine learning to rote-learning.

Discourages 'hard' academic subjects

The factory exam system incentivises schools to drop hard subjects and options that seem to be more difficult, and concentrate on those where passes are easier. The last 10 years has thus been a retreat from subjects such as mathematics, sciences, history and modern languages in favour of 'soft' subjects such as media studies, psychology and sociology. Although 75% of A-Levels are taken at non-selective state schools or colleges, 93% of media studies exams are taken there and 98% of sociology courses. Meanwhile, between 1997 and 2006, A-Level entries for maths fell by 18%, and for physics by 11%.[7]

As much a test of the school and the teachers as of candidates
Students in a school which has strong discipline and an excellent work ethic, and where teachers have 'cracked the code' of the exam game, will achieve far higher passes at GCSE and A-Level than those in schools that do not enjoy these benefits. This is a shocking truth, and one that perpetuates disadvantage and social exclusion.

In 2010, the British examination system is like the Austro-Hungarian empire 100 years before: crumbling apart, incoherent and unfit for purpose.

Alternative Models to A-Levels and GCSEs
Britain in 2010 is witnessing the break-up of the 'one size fits all' national examination system of A-Levels and GCSEs. A significant step was when Prime Minister Tony Blair announced at the SSAT conference in November 2006 that he wanted every educational authority to offer the International Baccalaureate. The arrival of Gordon Brown in Number 10 and of Ed Balls in the DCSF in June 2007, saw a shift away from IB back in favour of A-Levels and GCSEs, as well as championing of '14-19 Diplomas'.

The Conservatives have indicated that they will allow schools to decide the sort of exams they run, and it is clear that they are thinking in particular about the International GCSE (iGCSE) and

---

[7] Anna Fazackerley and Julian Chant, *The Hard Truth about 'soft' subjects,* Policy Exchange, December 2008.

the IB diploma. This new freedom is only to be granted if it allows for more academic rigour.

14-19 Diplomas

These were launched in September 2008, and offer students a combination of vocational and academic learning. However, despite intensive promotion, they have proved to be unloved, unpopular and lacking in academic credibility. Several top schools and universities have shunned them.[8] The Conservatives believe that the Diploma model is overly bureaucratic and have indicated that they will not let it continue in its current format.

The IGCSE

These were developed by University of Cambridge International Examinations and were launched in September 1985, and are now taken in 125 different countries. They are in effect GCSEs, but without modular exams. As they are seen to be more rigorous than conventional GCSEs, they have become increasingly popular with independent schools.

Despite the 'international' in the title, however, and their wide popularity throughout the world, there is nothing specifically international about them. The media, nevertheless, has portrayed schools choosing to sit them as taking a brave and a radical departure from the 'broken GCSEs'.

---

[8] Advertising Standards Authority Adjudications: Department for Children, Schools and Families, 28 October 2009. This upheld a complaint against the DCSF which had promoted the Diplomas in an advertisement which, in the words of the ASA, 'implied all Diplomas represented a level of academic qualification that would be accepted by all universities. Because that was not the case, we concluded the ads were misleading.'

The International Baccalaureate

The IB diploma was first developed in 1968 and has steadily increased in British schools and around the world. It is more intellectually rigorous than A-Level, has seen zero grade inflation, has terminal rather than modular exams, requires six subjects to be studied in depth (rather than three or four as in A-Level), involves students writing an extended project and them sitting a 'theory of knowledge' paper that examines critical thinking.[9]

A principal reason for the absence of grade inflation in the IB is that individual subjects and papers cannot be retaken, and the exam is not subject to political influence from any government.[10] The 'middle years programme' was developed in 1994, and it is for pupils from the age of pupils age 11 to 16 (Years 7 to 11). The 'primary years programme' was developed in 1997 and is proving to be increasingly popular with both state primary and independent prep schools.

The Cambridge 'Pre U'

This was developed in 2008 by University of Cambridge International Examinations. Concerned by the loss of rigour in A-Levels, it joined forces with a number of leading academic schools to produce this new qualification. The Pre-U has terminal exams at the end of the upper sixth, does not offer modules, and all candidates write an independent research essay. It is still, however, fundamentally the same structure to A-

---

[9] The *Education Briefing Book 2008* (Durham University, 2008) shows the diverging pass rates of the IB (stable) and A-Level (rapidly rising).

[10] E-mail from Patrick Watson to Anthony Seldon, 3 January 2010.

Level. Approximately 80 schools are said to offer the Pre-U and about 1,700 students will take the first Pre U exam in 2010.[11]

The Standardised Aptitude Test, or SAT
Until 2005 this was called the Scholastic Aptitude Test. It is a US exam which is growing in popularity in Britain. First introduced in 1901, it is used to determine whether or not a student is ready for college, and their level of ability in mathematics, critical reading, in writing, and in a selection of other subjects.

The Advanced Placement Programme (AP Programme)
This is another US exam which has growing interest in Britain. It was developed after 1945 by three of the top schools in the US, Lawrenceville, Phillips Exeter and Phillips Andover, together with Harvard, Princeton and Yale universities. The exam can be taken in a variety of subjects as students finish school and is regarded as an excellent preparation for university.

Assessing schools
The first school inspectors were appointed in 1833. Initially they had no or few guidelines to follow and judged schools according to their own professional experience.[12] Inspections have traditionally been feared by schools. But in recent years the trepidation they inspired reached new levels.

An inspection regime is of course a necessary longstop in any system to detect and root out corruption, poor standards and maladministration. Inspection can help in the following ways:

---

[11] Personal correspondence with University of Cambridge International Examinations, 24 November 2009.

[12] John Macbeath, *School inspection and self evaluation,* Routledge, 2006.

- To ensure that schools perform at the highest possible level.
- To identify weaknesses and suggest programmes for improvement.
- To provide information to parents and other interested parties.
- To ensure schools provide a minimum standard.
- To ensure that schools comply with legal requirements.

Used sensitively, and with discrimination, inspections can be therefore be helpful to a school, students and parents.

The traditional way of assessing schools has been through inspection. The school inspectorate and is overseen in England and Wales by the Office for Standards in Education (Ofsted) while in Scotland, schools are inspected by Her Majesty's Inspectorate, which is a branch of the Scottish Executive, and in Northern Ireland the Department of Education inspects schools.

Concerns with the Inspection regime

The inspection regime has been criticised from a number of, often contradictory, viewpoints over the last ten years:

They can be counterproductive

Inspections can induce an unnecessary degree of fear and stress for teachers and schools. This cannot be conducive to a fair and balanced assessment. Rather than being seen as constructive and helpful, they can make teachers defensive, less willing to listen, and unable or unwilling to perform at their natural level or best. Head teacher Geoff Barton wrote in January 2010 'instead of leaving each school wiser at the end of an inspection about how it might improve itself, too often experienced heads in good schools are battered'.[13] Gerard

---

[13] Geoff Barton, *Times Educational Supplement*, 1 January 2010.

Kelly, editor of the *TES*, said that Ofsted did not 'have a good year' in 2009 and accused it of 'behaving like a traffic warden'.[14]

Superficial
The inspection process can be a superficial view of the highly complex life of a school, which cannot be reduced to key indicators in the same way that a commercial organisation can with economic indicators and ratios. Inspectors have been criticised for basing their statements and judgements far too much on test results with too little on evidence gathered during the inspection.[15] A Centre for Policy Studies report recommended that Ofsted 'should focus exclusively on inspecting failing schools. More attention should be given to classroom inspection and less to desk analysis.'[16]

Chris Woodhead denounced inspections in May 2009 as 'an irrelevance these days. The inspectors spend a few minutes in the classrooms, they don't see every teacher teach, it is an exercise driven by the analysis of data'.[17] Barry Sheerman, chairman of the House of Commons select committee for schools, has criticised Ofsted for relying far too heavily on statistics. 'People in schools feel aggrieved. They may have

---

[14] Gerard Kelly, 'Unpopular is understandable – unfair is not,' *Times Educational Supplement*, 27 November 2009.

[15] Anastasia de Waal, *Inspection, Inspection, Inspection! How Ofsted crushes independent schools and independent teachers*, (London, 2006).

[16] Burkard and Talbot Rice, op. cit.

[17] 'Ofsted is part of the problem in education system, says Chris Woodhead', *The Times*, 23 May 2009. See also his powerful elegy, *A Desolation of Learning*, Pencil-Sharp Publishing, 2009.

worked their socks off... They find that all that really matters is how many GCSEs, [the children] have got and what level'.[18]

Unthinking compliance
Inspection can encourage the 'factory school' mentality and stifle individuality by making schools re-orientate themselves around what inspectors require. This can suppress creativity and individual approaches. Anastasia de Waal suggests that:[19]

> 'Ofsted degrades teachers. Under the current education regime, teachers are automatons not professionals. The criteria for a good inspection report push aside talent, innovation and good outcomes in favour of standardised procedures.'

Inspections are too removed
School inspectors have experiences often far removed from teachers. The idea of a team of inspectors, who are better paid than teachers (the average salary of inspectors has risen 38% between 2002 and 2008) rolling into schools and telling them what to do is found by many to be distasteful.[20]

The Independent Schools Inspectorate (ISI), founded in its present guise in 1998 has used serving teachers as inspectors

---

[18] 'Focus on under performing pupils damages the most able, say MPs', *The Daily Telegraph*, 22 November 2009.

[19] Anastasia de Waal, *Inspection, Inspection, Inspection!*, Civitas, 2006.

[20] Burkard and Talbot Rice, op. cit.

who know and understand the schools they are trying to assess. This system is clearly preferable.[21]

League Tables

Only a generation ago, hardly any state schools published their pupils' examination results. The absence of any comparative information was damaging to accountability and prevented parents, pupils and teachers making informed choices on school acheivements.

League tables were adopted in 1988 for secondary schools and in 1991 for primary and were soon eagerly published in national and local newspapers. Complaints about 'raw' league tables, which make no allowance for the ability of the intake, were met to some extent by more sophisticated 'value added' and 'contextual value added' league tables introduced in 2002 and 2006. Despite the coming of 'added value' tables, little or no allowance is made by the media for the quality of the intake.

State schools have no option but to be included in league tables, but some independent schools have been opting out of them since 2008 for two distinct reasons: those like Eton and St Paul's School for boys are so clearly at the top that they find the process demeaning while others refuse to participate because they feel that no allowance is made for their having lesser ability children, and therefore they feel stigmatised for appearing in the lower reaches of the table.

---

[21] Having been an ISI inspector since the pilot schemes in 1994, I have seen the 'peer-review' element as a core value of the independent school inspections system.

However idealistic a head teacher, and a school and the teachers within it, the fact that a state school's academic performance will get published each summer in the press, and that parents and outsiders will be making judgements on the school on that basis, is too powerful a force for any head or governing body not to be affected by. Criticisms of league tables include:

They cause damage and offence

Raw league tables make no allowance for academic ability of the intake, and therefore are above all a statement of the obvious. The media ignore this fact. It may well be the case, and often is the case, that schools with lower ability intakes will be doing far more to add value than those schools, often metropolitan, that are highly selective but which do far less to bring on their children academically. But they receive no reward in the raw league tables for their efforts: rather, a slap in the face.

They narrow schools

League tables reward only the performance at exams, and therefore skew schools towards exam teaching to the detriment of the all round academic education of a child, as well as to the detriment of the broader education of their whole 'eight aptitudes'. The treadmill of modular exams at GCSE and A-Level induces an unwelcome stranglehold on schools, putting them on an almost permanent 'war footing' as they prepare for exams.

Teaching exams, not subjects

Within academic subjects, they skew lessons away from the teaching of the subjects towards instruction of exam technique and mark maximisation. Teachers are almost forced to teach history GCSE rather than history, French AS-Level rather than French and physics A-Level rather than physics. The difference might sound slight, but it is in fact profound.

Modules handicap, not assist, learning
League tables encourage schools to take modules throughout the school year so that the pupils can pile up their exam marks, even though most teachers acknowledge that it is not in the interests of the students' academic development. It is a very brave school indeed which resists the sitting of modules. A shining example is Radley, an independent school in Oxfordshire, where the students do not sit any AS or A2 modules until the final summer term of the upper sixth.

Discriminate against academic subjects
They encourage the taking of 'easy subjects' such as art and drama, and militate against subjects such as mathematics and modern languages which are technically difficult.

Detract attention from the ability poles
The focus on pupils gaining at least a C grade in GCSE is resulting in the highest and lowest achievers being neglected. The House of Commons schools select committee concluded in November 2009 that 'staff feel under pressure to focus their attention on pupils who could receive a C grade and improve a schools league table standing at the expense of other pupils who might otherwise be able to gain an A or A*'.[22] A 'Teach First' report also concluded that 'the current system... focuses schools on getting results, rather than on helping individual pupils to achieve their potential'.[23]

---

[22] 'Focus on under performing pupils damages the most able, says MPs', *The Daily Telegraph*, 22 November 2009.

[23] Teach First, *Lessons from the Front*, November 2009.

Some conclusions on assessment in inspection

Central government does have responsibility for ensuring the efficient and rigorous inspection of schools; and of ensuring that the publication of data on school performance is genuinely useful for parents and others to make discriminating judgements.

But this responsibility must not infringe on the indepence of schools. So it is important that, while schools which are performing poorly should be inspected regularly, those performing at high levels should not be inspected at all.

6. TEACHERS AND LEADERS

Dilemma

The teaching profession requires teachers who are intellectually able, with the highest personal and ethical standards, willing to work long hours and in an environment where they must primarily rely upon their integrity and self-evaluation rather than the validation and approval of peers. The profession will never be able to attract individuals for the pay alone because doing so would require spending levels which would place an intolerable burden on taxpayers, and price independent schools out of existence.

How does one thus create an environment and way of life where those of the highest ability and dedication are willing to give their lives to teaching, and doing so for material rewards far less than their talents and industry might have brought them in other professions or in business life? How equally can one create an environment where highly talented and hard-working individuals want to run schools with all the sacrifices to their personal lives that school leadership entails, again for financial rewards far lower than leaders earn running similarly sized organisations in commercial life?

The joys of teaching

Teaching could be the most popular profession in the country. It is rare to meet someone without an opinion about teachers and schools, and many have, or had, hankerings to become teachers.

The attractions of teaching include:

- Few careers offer the same opportunities to influence for the better the lives of young people and where one knows one is making a real difference.
- One works alongside other individuals who have high ethical values and who are fired by a common sense of the public good.
- One is able to continue deepening a lifelong interest in the subject or subjects that one chose to study at university.
- It offers unrivalled opportunities to continue personal enthusiasms by coaching the young in their favoured activities, be it sport, drama, music, creative writing, outdoor adventure, faith work, and pastoral care.
- Pastoral care of students is emotionally deeply satisfying for teachers.
- There is job security, and long holidays (an entitlement of 12 weeks a year in the state sector, and up to 18 weeks a year in the independent sector).
- There are excellent opportunities for those seeking promotion to become academic or pastoral leaders, assistant or deputy heads, and heads or 'super-heads'.

Soluble problems with teaching and leading

Academic quality

While academic brilliance or originality is not absolutely necessary for good teaching, the profession is still not attracting sufficient numbers of high achieving graduates. A recent report observed that entry levels for English teachers are lower than in most other developed countries:[1]

> 'In general England's standard of entry is significantly lower on completion. For a secondary teaching post official requirements in England do not require the same standard of subject specialism as other countries do.'

The official requirements to become a teacher in England and Wales are C grades at GCSE English and Maths and a degree. At primary school, teacher qualifications and UCAS point requirements can be even lower: 41% of those entering a teacher training course had less than a 2:1 degree in 2005-06.

Deficiency of subject specialists
Experienced graduates are disproportionately found in the independent sector. A 2008 report found that independent school teachers were 'more likely than state school teachers to possess post-graduate qualifications, and to be specialists in shortage subjects.'[2] Yet state school students need subject specialists in mathematics, physics, and modern languages every bit as much as do students at independent schools.

---

[1] Sheila Lawlor et al, *Teachers Matter: Recruitment, Employment and Retention at home and abroad,* Politeia, 2009.

[2] Francis Green, Stephen Machin, Richard Murphy, Yu Zhu, *Competition for private and state school teachers,* Centre for the Economics of Education, LSE, January 2008.

Inadequate training in Teacher Training Colleges

Training of teachers at Teacher Training Colleges remains unsatisfactory. When I trained as a teacher 25 years ago taking a Postgraduate Certificate of Education (PGCE), the one point on which fellow students agreed was that the most valuable element was teaching in the classroom, and sharing these experiences with other trainee teachers. The least valuable aspect was the theory studied in college.

Things have got worse since then in Teacher Training Colleges. The six year DCSF report *Becoming a Teacher* found that 46% of BEd students thought their courses "too theoretical" as did 19% of secondary PGCE students.[3] Many said that what they were being taught in college made little real impact on their own teaching or the issues that arise in the classroom: one summed it up 'enough about that theory and that theory, tell me how I mark a child's book.'[4]

Attrition

Unacceptably high drop-out rates continue in the profession: between a third and a half of teachers drop out either during training or during their first three years of work, over double the rates of France and Germany.5 The reasons for teachers dropping out in Britain are given as 'a heavy workload along with too many government reforms, poor pupil behaviour,

---

[3]   A J Hobson et al, *Becoming a Teacher: Student teachers' experiences of initial teacher training in England*, DfES.

[4]   *More Good Teachers*. Michael Marland's slim volume *The Craft of the Classroom,* first published in 1975, contains all that a trainee teacher needs to know about teaching and managing students.

[5]   *Teachers Matter.*

general stress, and feeling 'undervalued". In January 2010 it was revealed that 25,000 who had qualified since the year 2000 have left full-time teaching in state schools, without even entering the classroom.6

Needless bureaucracy
Teachers are required to spend too much of their time on clerical jobs and bureaucracy. More clerical support would certainly help teachers, but more important would be a huge reduction in bureaucracy, much of it unnecessary and generated by central government. Teachers' time needs to be freed up to allow them to concentrate on preparation, teaching and marking, their three main academic responsibilities. There are now believed to be approximately 175,600 Teaching Assistants; in many cases they are well used, in many cases they are not. Some have suggested that up to 40,000 could be dismissed, and the money redeployed for more teachers.[7]

Obstacles to mature aspirants
The Government claims that 70% of enquiries about becoming teachers are now coming from mature graduates considering a career switch.[8] Much of this enthusiasm is however needlessly sacrificed. Pathways into teaching can be overly complicated for those who want to join the profession in their 30s, 40s, and 50s.

---

[6] 'Hundreds of thousands of qualified teachers not working in profession', *The Times*, 1 January 2010.

[7] 'Schools are wasting millions, says leaked report', *The Guardian*, 27 September 2009.

[8] *The Sunday Times*, 3 January 2010.

Three facets are required for a good teacher: the ability, the will and the training. If an individual has the will to teach, and the personal and communication qualities, they can usually pick up the training quickly on the job and do not need to spend a whole year of their lives, in expensive and often otiose college training. Chris Woodhead encapsulates it:[9]

> 'Allow those who in mid career want to become teachers to enter the profession without having to waste (and fund) a year's training'.

80% of managers and professionals who were interested in entering teaching said that they were more likely to do so if there were a fast track system.[10] Such a programme, called 'teach next', is widely supported.[11] 'Teach First' a programme developed by Tony Blair and Andrew Adonis to recruit exceptional graduates for challenging schools positions, began to place its first graduates in 2003. By 2009, 485 graduates were participating in the scheme, which is making a real difference. The programme needs to be extended considerably.

De-professionalisation

The professionalism and autonomy of the teacher has been steadily eroded. John McIntosh, formerly head of the state school London Oratory, said 'teachers are simply not professionals anymore, it has become a profession of

---

[9]   *Teachers Matters.*

[10]   *More good teachers.*

[11]   Ibid. Julia Margo, Meghan Barton, Kay Withers, Sonia Sodha, *Those who can?*, Institute for Public Policy Research, 2008.

managers, who manage according to a government plan.'[12] Independent school head Diane Watkins asserts:[13]

> 'The enthusiasm and sheer love of teaching which we all remember from our best experiences of school, seems to have been suppressed. It is as if teaching has become a management task where spontaneity, passion and enchantment have been lost.'

She expresses a concern, shared by many, that teacher training colleges tend to churn out factory teachers, rather than independent-minded professionals. A profound commitment to Continuous Professional Development (CPD) is in the DNA of all successful companies, as it is of flourishing schools. Yet for many years, teachers' CPD money and time has been given over to courses on exam techniques or understanding the government's curriculum and assessment reforms.14

A collective failure of moral courage
There has been a long-standing reluctance among the profession to acknowledge poor practice. Most heads and teachers recognise the phenomenon all too well: everyone in the staff room knows who the poor and the lazy teachers are and everyone grumbles about them. So to do the students, and often so do the parents. The leadership is often blamed for a failure to grip the problem.

---

[12] Interview with researcher, 1 October 2009.

[13] Comments to author, September 2009.

[14] *More good teachers.*

But as soon as the management takes action, other teachers start to defend their unsatisfactory colleagues and accuse the school leadership of brutality. Yet the continuance of poor teachers and poor teaching does untold damage to schools. Pupils taught by the worst teachers learn four times less than those taught by the best.[15] Other research suggests that the ramifications of having a poor teacher in the reception year at school were still detectable six years later and affected SATs performance.[16] And it has been found that pupils who are taught by the worst teachers get at least a grade lower at GCSE than those taught by the best.[17] Eric Hanushek reaches similar conclusions about the US. He concludes that the teacher makes all the difference, and that a class with a good teacher can learn a year and a half's material versus the half a year of work that a poor teacher gets through in a school year.[18]

Despite this clear evidence on the importance of teacher quality, the General Teaching Council for England (GTC), the professional body to improve the quality of teaching and the standards among teachers, has failed sufficiently to champion good teaching and penalise poor teaching. In August 2009, it was

---

[15] 'Invest in teachers to raise achievement', Institute of Education website, 2 April 2009.

[16] Peter Tymms, Paul Jones, Stephen Albone, Brian Henderson, 'The First Seven Years at school' in *Educational Assessment, Evaluation and Accountability*, February 2009.

[17] Helen Slater, Simon Burges, Neil Davies, *Do teachers matter? Measuring the variation in teacher effectiveness in England*, Bristol University, January 2009.

[18] Eric Hanushek, *Schoolhouses, Courthouses, and Statehouses: Solving the Funding-Achievement Puzzle in America's Public Schools*, Princeton University Press, 2009.

revealed that 75% of complaints to the GTC are dismissed with no further investigation.[19] This a major part of the problem: only eight teachers were barred by the GTC between 2001 and 2008.[20]

How many poor teachers are there? Chris Woodhead has estimated that there might be as many as 15,000 and Cyril Taylor as many as 17,000.[21] Both were widely castigated for saying what they said. Yet it is the students who continue to suffer.

Inadequate support for leadership
School leadership is not as good as it should be in Britain. And the problem could get worse: a third of all current head teachers were expected to retire between 2008 and 2012.[22]

School leadership should be an immensely rewarding career, with the potential to make a real difference for the better for a vast number of lives. Yet heads complain that the quality of their work is damaged by excessive bureaucracy, limited autonomy, and high stress, and as a result job satisfaction is far lower than it should be.

---

[19] 'Headteachers: '75% of complaints to GTC are dismissed', *Times Educational Supplement*, 14 August 2009.

[20] See Sam Freedman, Briar Lipson *Slipping Through the Net: Tackling incompetence in the teaching profession*, Policy Exchange, 2008.

[21] '17,000 teachers not up to the job says head of standards body', *The Guardian,* 2 February 2008.

[22] National College of School Leadership, *Annual Accounts, 2008/09.*

Some recommendations on teaching and leadership

Pathways into teaching should be made easier for able and highly committed graduates. There should be less emphasis on theory for postgraduates, and easier entry into teaching for those who have already built careers outside the profession. 'Teach First' has helped make the profession more attractive, and needs to become 'Teach Second' and 'Teach Third'.

As with teachers, school leaders need practical experience not an excess of theory proffered by people who are not themselves leaders and understand little of the reality of school life. The job of leadership is simple to state; it is to develop a vision, to communicate that vision, appoint and motivate those who will deliver the vision, and then to monitor its success and amend the vision as necessary.

7. ORGANISATION AND STRUCTURES

Dilemma

The independent sector demonstrates that schools flourish when they are challenged in the marketplace and when they are given high degrees of independence to succeed, or fail.

But how, in a world where schools are significantly free of central direction and oversight, does one ensure that the lazy, the incompetent and the malign will not take over those schools, allowing standards to fall? Schools give children a once in a lifetime opportunity to develop, and if liberty becomes licence to be mediocre, young people's opportunities will be forever damaged, and government will have failed to ensure that each child receives the standard of education they all should have.

Academies 1989-2010

The Blair Government did do much to increase the autonomy of state schools. The strategy was led by Andrew Adonis, who seized on the idea of City Technology Colleges (CTCs) started under Thatcher in 1989. These morphed into 'city academies', and then just plain 'academies'. These 'independent state schools' were pushed by Blair and Adonis in the face of a deeply sceptical Chancellor of the Exchequer, Gordon Brown.

Towards the end of Blair's premiership, in his SSAT speech in Birmingham in November 2006, he announced that the target for academies was to rise from 200 to 400, without having secured prior Treasury agreement.[1] When Brown succeeded Blair in June 2007, appointing his key policy adviser Ed Balls in charge of schools, the expectation was that academy momentum would dwindle, especially as they had provoked the ire of both the teaching unions and local authorities. Some freedoms for academies, such as over the curriculum, were taken away, to howls of protest, but the educational world was surprised to find Brown and Balls themselves latter day converts to academies.

The Conservatives have been vocal champions of extending academies across the state sector. They highlight signal successes such as Mossbourne Academy which opened in 2004 in Hackney, East London under the sponsorship of philanthropist Clive Bourne and the dedicated leadership of capable head Sir Michael Wilshaw. There, a rigorous approach to learning and a strict discipline policy have helped to produce extremely high (85% A*-C) GCSE results, especially impressive as 40% of its intake are on Free School Meals (FSM).[2] The Conservatives have decided to push far ahead of Labour in the granting of autonomy to schools.

Michael Gove is the direct successor of Lord Adonis, and is unafraid of championing the achievements of this high priest of New Labour policy. Drawing heavily on the experience of

---

[1]   'Blair wants another 200 academies', BBC website, 30 November 2006, Anthony Seldon, *Blair Unbound*, Simon & Schuster, 2007.

[2]   'The case for academies', The Guardian, 8 September 2009. See also Mossbourne Academy website www.mossbourne.hackney.sch.uk/

'charter schools' in the US and the 'free schools' in Sweden, as well as on the extensive evidence compiled by James Tooley and others of the growth and success of independent schools around the world, Gove has come up with a brave programme to extend school autonomy.[3] He proposes to remove any powers over schools that local authorities continue to hold, transferring it directly to the schools themselves. Schools shall also be given the option of choosing the exams that they believe educationally appropriate for them within the context of a slimmed down National Curriculum. Gove proposes three routes for enhancing school independence: an existing school sponsors a new school; an existing school judged 'outstanding' by Ofsted may become an academy: finally, a group of individuals can set up their own school, provided they make a convincing business case, can produce a convincing plan, and can prove that there is a demand for such a school.

These proposals envisage freedoms for all schools similar to those that the existing academies possess including restoring freedoms removed by Brown after 2007. But their plans fall a long way short of giving state schools the freedoms currently enjoyed by independent schools. They will not become legally independent entities. They will not be free to select their own pupils but will have to follow existing admissions codes that

---

[3]   James Tooley, *The Beautiful Journey: A Personal Journey into How the World's Poorest People are Educating Themselves*, Cato Institute, 2009. 'Will lessons from America be lost in translation?', *Times Educational Supplement*, 11 December 2009. Note that critics point out that the international examples are not conclusive: for example, a Stanford University Study has shown that 37% of charter schools gave pupils a 'significantly worse' education than standard state schools, and only 17% delivered a better education – while 46% made little or no difference. However, Charter Schools in New York out-perform their peers (*New York Times,* 10 January 2010).

dictate that they may decide no more than 10% of admissions according to the specialism of the school. There is no disguising the fact that, under the Conservatives proposed model, schools would remain more 'state' than 'independent'.

In January 2010, Britain had 200 academies. Tory sources suggest that by 2014/5, there may be '1000 or more academies or free schools'. This development is in line with what many state school heads themselves want.[4] Typical of state school heads is Peter Barnes of Oakgrove school in Milton Keynes, who says that the freedoms that independent school heads enjoy that he would most relish are:

- not having to respond to government initiatives e.g. on 'national strategies' and on diplomas;
- being able to select more of his students who have strengths in his school's specialism;
- greater freedom to direct his staff as he thinks fit, e.g. for exam cover;
- greater freedom over exclusions (though independent schools are themselves subject to elaborate appeals processes on exclusions).5

Criticism of academies

Academies are not without their critics, from both left- and right-of-centre sources. Education journalist Warwick Mansell in December 2009 criticised the sheer expense of the academy programme, arguing that it has not received the sponsorship

---

[4] A survey, conducted in March/April 2009 for an earlier version of this report, found 70% of those who responded said they favoured greater autonomy in their schools.

[5] Telephone conversation with Peter Barnes, 21 December 2009.

from the private sector that was originally the programme's main selling point: the 200 academies established so far have received only two-thirds of the £145 million in capital funding that they were due from sponsors.[6]

A recent report cast serious doubts upon the academic claims for academies.[7] It points out that many academies have refused to disclose the subjects that pupils take at GCSE because they are not bound by the terms of the Freedom of Information Act. Some of the academies they investigated encouraged students to take fewer academic subjects in order to boost their GCSE grades. They even go as far as to recommend the immediate suspension of further academies pending an investigation. Chris Woodhead in early 2010 has challenged Michael Gove head on, saying that the success of schools like Mossbourne is nothing to do with them being academies: 'They succeed because they are led by an outstanding head teacher'.[8]

Further organisational issues
Independence for schools, once established, would reduce greatly the role for Local Education Authorities (LEAs). In particular, LEAs would lose all control over both school funding and schools admissions. Councils could, if they wished, continue to offer support services to schools, to help them with school management or other matters. However, they would have no monopoly right to provide these services. Schools would

---

[6] 'Are academies just a 'ludicrously expensive con-trick'?', *The Guardian*, 1 December 2009.

[7] Anastasia de Waal, *The Secrets of Academies Success*, Civitas, December 2009.

[8] *Standpoint*, January/February 2010.

have the right to buy them from whatever source they wanted, including the private sector or from a neighbouring council if they wished. Any council would only be able to succeed in the provision of these activities if they could persuade enough schools that they provided them effectively.

Local authorities would continue to hold some relevant functions. These would include activities such as child protection and administration of children with special education needs, and ensuring that all children get a full-time education. These roles could be transferred to the local social services departments.

Streaming, setting and academic selection
A strong educational case can be made for school selection at 14 and it is one that is being heard more loudly.[9] Selection at 14 has some advantages over selection at the age of 11, because children mature considerably between the ages of 11 and 14, and their academic potential has been given much more opportunity to flower. Whatever the merits of a 14+ exam, and it is attracting some powerful advocates, redesigning schools to create academic and vocational colleges for 14 to 18 year olds is also unlikely, not the least in the current economic climate.

What is much more immediately practical is academic streaming and setting *within existing schools* from the age of 11 (as happens in some state schools and almost all independent schools).[10] The academic evidence points very clearly in its favour. There are profound merits for schools to be divided into

---

[9]   Geoff Lucas 'Why is 'selection' still such a dirty word?', *Times Educational Supplement*, 30 January 2009.

[10]   In streaming, children are grouped by ability for all subjects, in setting only by specific subjects, most commonly for maths.

top, middle and lesser academic streams, and additionally setting for subjects e.g. science (which tests the logical intelligence) and modern languages (which tests linguistic intelligence).

School size

While no ideal school size for all exists, some schools can be too small to allow for the full range of opportunities for students and teachers, while others can be too big, militating against students being known as individuals. While 'all-age' schools can successfully be bigger in size because they are effectively made up of separate sections, (i.e. nursery/primary/secondary), state schools in general today tend to be too big, above all at secondary level.

In England and Wales, there are 18,509 maintained primary schools, with an average size of 224; and there are 3,448 state secondary schools, with an average pupil population of 975.[11] One of the great advantages of the independent sector has over state schools is smaller scale, which is further enhanced by the far more generous teacher:pupil ratio and the breaking down of large schools into smaller units (or 'houses'). Eton is the largest independent boarding school in Britain with just over 1,300 pupils, but it works well because it is broken down into 24 separate houses (and one additional 'college').

Schools need to have a human scale, where not just the students but also the parents are known as individuals. Contrast the Finnish system of education, consistently rated one of the

---

[11] Anna Riggell and Caroline Sharp, *The Structure of Primary Education*, Primary Review, NFER, 2008. DCSF data compiled from statistics available at: http://www.dcsf.gov.uk/rsgateway/DB/SFR/s000843/index.shtml

finest in the world, where schools rarely exceed 700 pupils, and children are often taught by the same teachers for three or four years at a time.[12]

Where it is impossible for secondary schools to be smaller than 1000, schools can be broken up to contain smaller sub-schools within them, so that each child has a smaller unit with which to identify. Crown Woods School in Eltham South London, for example, under its re-organisation plan, will be divided into three separate colleges for 11 to 16 year olds and a separate Sixth Form, with no unit exceeding 450.[13] The enterprising Head, Michael Murphy, drawing on the experience of smaller schools in the US, wanted his students and parents to be known individually to teachers. One of the colleges will allow high ability pupils a 'fast track' curriculum, the sort of streamed education hitherto only available to grammar school pupils.[14] Another school to have benefited from this thinking is Brislington Enterprise College in Bristol, which was rebuilt around "houses" for 250-300 students: GCSE results have improved dramatically at the school.[15] Such strategies need to be implemented on a much wider scale if children are to be given the personalised education they deserve.

---

[12] John Abbott, *A Briefing Paper for Parliamentarians on the Design Flaws at the Heart of English Education*, 21st Century Learning Initiative, 2009.

[13] Letter from head teacher to Anthony Seldon, 5 December 2009.

[14] 'Building Schools for the Future', 3 September 2009.

[15] Brislington's story is told in Wendy Wallace, *Schools within Schools*, Calouste Gulbenkian Foundation, 2009.

Parental involvement

Research shows a clear correlation between parental involvement and academic achievement of students, although it is difficult, for obvious reasons, to prove a causal link.[16] Some schools are far more successful at achieving high levels of parental involvement than others. Independent schools see close parental interest and support for their children's academic progress, explained perhaps by higher average aspiration and educational levels of independent school parents, and because they have chosen the school and are making financial sacrifices.

When a consumer is not given a choice, it is inevitable that what is on offer will be valued less highly; if parents are told what state school their child is to attend, and if there is no financial commitment, there are fewer grounds for parents feeling an active commitment. Giving all parents a choice of their children's school, and indeed allowing them to pay (to be discussed in the next chapter), are the longer term solutions.

In the immediate term, parents' contracts have been shown to be effective in ensuring attendance at parents' evenings, support for school rules and homework, and an absence of intimidation or threats to the school and its teachers. In the longer run, subtler methods need to be introduced to nudge parents voluntarily to take a closer interest in their children's schooling. A mark of a successful head is the degree of parental buy-in and loyalty they achieve in their school.

---

[16] W H Jeynes, *Parental involvement and student achievement: A meta-analysis,* Family Involvement Research Digest, Harvard, 2007.

Governing bodies

Many schools, state and independent, find it hard to recruit governors, and specifically, those with relevant experience (finance, law, personal management) and with the time to devote to schools. Conversely, heads can find themselves overly encumbered by governing bodies, and would prefer to be given a wider measure of freedom.[17]

When governing bodies do not work well, two main factors are at play. They can be overly intrusive, detracting from a head's time, energy and even sapping their confidence; writing reports for governors, second guessing what can be capricious demands, attending governors' meetings and following up action points and queries can be highly time consuming. Many individual governors, and indeed governing bodies, do not understand fully the difference between governance, their own job, and executive leadership, the job of the head.

Secondly, governing bodies are traditionally weak at dealing with heads in difficulty. Where a good head is having problems governors need to offer steadfast support. But where a head is never going to make the grade, governing bodies can be slow to act, with the result that a weak head can continue in office and drag back a school. What heads need from governing bodies is financial oversight above all, guidance where appropriate on strategy, trust and tangible support by turning up at school's prestige events.

---

[17]   Anthony Seldon, *How Governors can be More Effective*, AGBIS lecture, 16 February 2009.

Co-education vs. single sex

Few subjects exercise more emotional energy than this question.[18] But if state schools are to become more independent, then this is exactly the sort of decision which should be left to the discretion of heads and governing bodies.

Alternative models for school organisation

There is already an extraordinarily wide range of different types of schools in Britain. Most of these are fairly small scale. But their existence suggests that, if independence for state schools is more widely granted, then even greater diversity will flourish.

Studio schools

Studio schools take their inspiration from Nobel Prizewinning author James Heckmann, who argued that employability skills are at least as important as technical skills in determining career success, earnings and success at work.[19] Studio schools are for 14-19 year olds, and are designed in particular for those who traditional schools have failed to motivate. Students spend part of each week in paid employment. The first wave of studio schools in Britain are to be opened in September 2010, in Blackpool, Kirklees, Lambeth, Luton, Newham, Oldham, and South Tyneside.

A variant of studio schools are technical schools, proposed by former Conservative education secretary Lord Baker.[20] Based

---

[18] The most exhaustive study of the whole co-ed vs. single sex debate concluded that single sex does offer the benefits its advocates believe. See Alan Smithers and Pamela Robinson, *The Paradox of Single-Sex and Co-educational Schooling*, 2006

[19] *What is a Studio School?*, Studio Schools Trust (undated).

[20] Lord Baker, 'Don't trivialise technical', *The House Magazine*, 10 November 2008.

on vocational skills, these technical colleges for 14 to 19 year olds would have 500 to 600 students each and would work closely with firms and businesses in the locality.[21] Lord Baker has argued that:

> 'Our secondaries do not have the space, equipment, or qualified staff to teach welding, bricklaying and so on... Germany has them and they are more popular than their grammar schools.'

These technical schools would become academies and already universities like Aston are interested in sponsoring them. Alan Smithers has advocated another variant, in a study funded by the Gatsby Charitable Foundation. He advocated specialist science schools able to select the brightest science pupils at the age of 14.[22] He believes that this reform is necessary in part to boost the numbers of students opting for science at A-Level, particularly physics.

Small schools
For many years, 'small schools' have been associated with the *avant garde*, such as Satish Kumar's 'The Small School' in Totnes, Devon, which has about 20 students. Some recent research has suggested that small schools can in fact be much more effective than larger schools in raising the young.[23]

---

[21] Lord Baker 'Why our children need the return of technical colleges', *Yorkshire Post*, 16 August 2008.

[22] Alan Smithers, *Study into the impact of science specialist schools on student performance in physics*, Gatsby Technical Education Projects, 2009.

[23] The Small School's website is http://www.thesmallschool.org.uk/index.html.

The New Model School Company

The think tank Civitas runs these not-for-profit schools, which include the Faraday School in London. They charge low fees, less than £2,000 a term, and rely upon the donations of altruistic investors. [24] The vast bulk of the income goes to teachers, which permits small class sizes (20 per class maximum), with up to three support teachers per classroom. The curriculum in these schools is fairly traditional, as is the pedagogic style, but there is an enhanced emphasis on creative subjects, which are taught in the afternoon.

The New Schools Network

This was established in October 2009 by Rachel Wolf, and seeks to set up individual and heavily autonomous schools, with the freedom to offer what parents want. [25] The approach is for head teachers to be given the power to determine all key decisions including class size, length of school day, and admissions criteria. Despite only being active for a few months, the Network has been 'inundated with queries' from 'hundreds of parents groups' indicating a real groundswell of opinion in favour of parental involvement in the schools system. [26]

Community Schools

Some schools, usually led by inspiring heads, open themselves up to the public, and make their facilities available to the whole

---

[24] The New Model School Company website is www.newmodelschool.co.uk/. See also 'New not-for-profit private school chain is a class apart', *Daily Telegraph,* 12 November 2009.

[25] The New Schools Network website is www.newschoolsnetwork.org

[26] 'Parents enticed by Tory plan for 'free schools'. *The Guardian,* 13 December 2009.

community. A radical example of this is in Knowsley on Merseyside where 11 secondary schools have been replaced by seven 'centres for learning'. One of their features is to open up to the public outside of school hours.[27] This reorganisation was overseen by Damian Allen, the executive director of the LEA, and is a shining example of what a dynamic local authority can achieve.

International schools

There are about 30 'international schools' in Britain. These are independent schools which have affiliations with countries abroad (for example the French Lycée Charles de Gaulle Londres, and The American School in London). Some purely British state schools are internationally-minded, such as Broadgreen International School in Liverpool, which offers the International Baccalaureate or Kingsford Community School in Newham, London, which has pioneered the teaching of Mandarin. The independent Sevenoaks School has been committed to internationalism for over 40 years, and where all students sit the IB diploma in the sixth form.

All British schools, whether state or independent, would benefit from developing a substantial international focus. British schools have much to learn from schools abroad.[28] School leaders have much to gain from understanding more clearly the problems faced by school leaders overseas. ICT offers unrivalled, and still

---

[27] 'Future Schooling Knowsley: a transformational learning strategy', BSF Case Studies: Education Vision, March 2009.

[28] It is one of the principal achievements of the Specialist Schools and Academies Trust (SSAT) to have built bridges between British schools and those overseas.

largely untapped opportunities to bring the world into the domain of each British school.

Boarding schools
Boarding schools offer considerable advantages, above all more time for purposeful activities, avoidance of time wasted daily on travel, the experience of self reliance, and security for children from difficult backgrounds or whose parents work antisocial hours or live abroad. The Royal Alexandra and Albert school in Surrey is the largest state boarding school in Britain and a first rate example of the benefits of boarding in state schools.

The school environment
Understanding of the linkage between the School's physical environment and the performance and wellbeing of its students is still in its infancy.[29]

A telling statement about the importance of present school design was provided by a Teachers Support Network survey in 2008. It found that 87% of the teachers they surveyed 'believed that school environments influence pupil behaviour', and that

---

[29] For example, a Newcastle University report (*School building programmes, motivations, consequences and implications,* 2005) recommended avoiding the dull uniformity of school design of the 1970s and 1980s, but concluded that the effect of architecture on children can be exaggerated. The Cambridge Primary Review (*The Built Environment,* 2008) highlighted the adverse impact on children of excessive noise, poor ventilation, and lack of exposure to natural light. The NFER surveyed the impact of the extensive 'Building Schools for the Future' programme *The effects of the school environment on young people's learning,* 2008) and noted positive results from younger children. It did however conclude that 'it is not possible to prove a "causal link" between the improved attitudes of the students and the move to the new BSF buildings'.

only 12% believed that current school buildings offered an effective learning environment.[30] With this widespread kind of discontent in mind, the 'Great Schools Inquiry' chaired by former education secretary Estelle Morris was set up in 2009 to explore what makes a great school for the 21st century.[31] The report is likely to conclude what every successful teacher knows in their bones: if you make your classroom and school in general attractive and welcoming, pupils will enjoy being in them, they will learn more, and have more pride in their school.

ICT and classrooms and schools for the future[32]

'Moore's law' suggests that computing power is taking off at an exponential rate, and is likely to continue to do so until 2015 at least. But, as of 2010, despite computers having been in schools for over thirty years, there is little clarity about how they will change teaching and learning in the future. What is reasonably clear is the benefits of ICT to date:

- It cuts administration costs, not the least by reducing photocopying bills and enhancing cheap intra-school communication.
- It facilitates home – school communication, allowing parents at a glance to understand what is happening at the school, how well their child is faring, and what exactly they are studying, as well as allowing students remote access through websites to learning resources.

---

[30] 'Memorandum submitted by Teacher Support Network and the British Council for School Environments (BCSE)', Teacher Support Network, 2 July 2008.

[31] Great Schools Inquiry, British Council for School Environments (www.bcse.uk.net)

[32] Great thanks to David Smith of St Paul's School for his guidance on this section.

- It facilitates independent learning with students researching online while remaining at their own desk.
- It allows schools to share resources.
- It can create far more dramatic and memorable lessons. Teachers further can share and store their own best material. Distance learning can be made available for students who might not have access to specialist teachers.
- It encourages enterprise and creative thinking among pupils. For example, in St Paul's School for boys students have set up a range of websites, including one that aggregates feedback about interviews at universities.

ICT can be used far better in schools. Many teachers' knowledge of ICT is considerably behind that of their students, while teachers' understanding of their students' mastery of multimedia ICT can be baleful. Stephen Heppell, a former ICT adviser to government, has since 2004 hosted the annual 'Be Very Afraid' forum at the BAFTA headquarters in London, an exhibition where school children show off their technological know-how and show adults how advanced is their understanding of computer technology.[33]

The following are the principal areas where ICT needs to be improved in schools:

- Greater investment and time is needed for teacher training, and training for management and leadership, so that they can galvanise what should be happening in their schools.
- More investment so that every classroom in Britain has an interactive whiteboard, and every child a laptop computer.

---

[33] Heppell's website is http://www.heppell.net/bva/

- Teachers need to understand how much their role has changed, and adapt to that change. A new emphasis is needed on understanding the process of learning which harnesses the power of digital participation between students and teachers.
- School libraries will never again be silent areas stuffed with books that few read, where students have to passively absorb the material of other minds. They need to be bright, airy spaces, with quieter areas where students can work on their own laptops, and more social areas where seating encourages to collaborative learning. Libraries could become places where students create and share their own resources. Schools should have much more open architecture: 'open plan' schools will become the norm.[34]
- Computer games such as *Portal*, should be celebrated, not shunned. Many such games require high level collaborative teamwork skills of a kind celebrated by many employers. They can help give students a feeling for physics and provide continuous assessment of their performance.[35]
- Project work, based on genuine original research, and free of plagiarism, needs to become much more common at schools, utilising the vast bank of information available on-line. The IB, and now Pre-U, offer extended essays: they should become far more common activities.

State and independent schools

On coming to power in 1997, Tony Blair promised to create 'world class' state schools, which would become so good that

---

[34] Stephen Heppell, 'Education is Dead, Long Live Learning', *Times Educational Supplement,* 1 January 2010.

[35] E-mail, David Smith to Anthony Seldon, 23 December 2009.

the middle classes would want to opt-out of paying for expensive independent education.

Today, despite 13 years of New Labour, two prime ministers who have given more personal attention to education than any previous incumbents at No. 10 of any party, a bigger increase in *per capita* spending on state schools than at any point in history, and despite having some bigger beasts in charge of schools than has been the norm before, the gulf in performance between independent and state schools is wider than ever.

The gulf in performance can be measured in terms of:

- Spending. Average fees per pupil in independent secondary schools are over £12,000 per year, compared to £4,600 – which rises to £6,000 per annum when revenues and capital are included – for a state secondary pupil.[36]
- Teacher:pupil ratios. There is one teacher to every 11 pupils in the independent sector compared to one to 17 in the state sector.[37]
- Educational performance. In Independent School Council (ISC) schools, 59.8% of GCSE entries resulted in an A/A* grade while at maintained schools the figure was 21.6%.[38]

---

[36] Anastasia de Waal, *Education in England: policy versus Impact*, Civitas, 2009. 'Private school fees 'kept down' in recession', *The Daily Telegraph*, 2 October 2009. Note the work of Nick Seaton in this field who has demonstrated the great difficulty of accurately measuring per pupil spending in the state sector.

[37] ISC, *ISC Census 2009*, 2009 and DCSF *School Workforce in England*, 2009.

[38] ISC, *GCSE Results*, www.isc.co.uk/FactsFigures_GCSEResults.htm

- School size. Over 75% of Independent School's Council (ISC) secondary schools have less than 750 pupils, compared to 55% of state secondary schools which have more than 900 pupils).[39]

Three conclusions can be drawn from 13 years of New Labour:

- The disparities in performance between the independent and state sectors are increasing, not reducing.
- Those children from the least advantaged backgrounds who would benefit from additional funding above the average, are receiving a worse education than those who attend popular state schools or who attend fee-paying schools.
- Independent schools have improved more rapidly than state schools. The existing mix of policies to deal with the divide between independent and state schools will never succeed in closing the gap.

The conclusion
A new approach is needed. Its ultimate aim must be independence for all schools.

---

[39] ISC, *ISC Census 2009*, 2009; 'Finding the best size for school', BBC, 15 September 2009.

ACKNOWLEDGEMENTS

My greatest debt is to Jonathan Meakin, who has been much more than a mere research assistant for the four months it has taken to write this booklet. He has been remarkably assiduous, hard working and imaginative and has improved the booklet enormously.

I would like to thank the following for reading all or parts of the book: Patrick Watson, Alan Smithers, Geoff Lucas, David James, Justin Garrick and Claire Robinson.

The following helped provide background information: John McIntosh, David Levin, Michael Bentley, Elizabeth Reid, Kathryn Ecclestone, James Turner, Nick Seaton, Steve Beswick and Ray Fleming, David Smith, Michael Barber, Ian Fordham, Dylan Wiliam, Peter Monteath, Oliver Marjot, Jessica Seldon, Alice Mosby, Ed Cooke, Greg Detre, Kevin Stannard, Jim Proce, Michael Murphy, Lys Johnson, Marcia Brophy and Anna Shandro.

This book is based on 25 years of experience of working in schools, I would like to thank all my colleagues and students, and most especially at Wellington College, whose experience was much in mind when I wrote this booklet.

Finally, I would like to thank Jill Kirby and Tim Knox at the Centre for Policy Studies for their indefatigable support during the writing of this report. I cannot thank them enough.

Anthony Seldon
1 January 2010.

BECOME AN ASSOCIATE OF
THE CENTRE FOR POLICY STUDIES

The Centre for Policy Studies is one of Britain's best-known and most respected think tanks. Independent from all political parties and pressure groups, it advocates a distinctive case for smaller, less intrusive government, with greater freedom and responsibility for individuals, families, business and the voluntary sector.

Through our Associate Membership scheme, we welcome supporters who take an interest in our work. Associate Membership is available for £100 a year (or £90 a year if paid by bankers' order). Becoming an Associate will entitle you to:

all CPS publications produced in a 12-month period

invitations to lectures and conferences

advance notice by e-mail of our publications, briefing papers and invitations to special events

For more details, please write or telephone to:
The Secretary
Centre for Policy Studies
57 Tufton Street, London SW1P 3QL
Tel: 020 7222 4488
Fax: 020 7222 4388
E-mail: mail@cps.org.uk
Website: www.cps.org.uk

Centre
for Policy
Studies

RECENT PUBLICATIONS

Be Bold For Growth
Paul Diggle and Paul Ormerod
"It is rare for economists to ask the right questions nowadays so a new pamphlet from the Centre for Policy Studies is welcome" – *Fund Manager*

Go for Growth: cut taxes now to cut debt
Michael Forsyth and Corin Taylor
"As the Centre for Policy Studies powerfully argued this week, cutting corporation tax to 20 per cent would be a much-needed spur to growth" – *leading article in The Spectator*

Wasted: the betrayal of white working class and black Caribbean boys
Harriet Sergeant
"I cannot remember when I last read something which inspired such exasperation, hopelessness and rage..." – Bruce Anderson, *The Independent*

Quantitative Easing: a history
George Trefgarne
'One of the most thorough and thoughtful investigations into the policy yet" – *The Daily Telegraph*

School quangos: a blueprint for abolition and reform
Tom Burkard and Sam Talbot Rice
"a compelling manifesto" – *The Spectator*